FEMININE ENERGY AWAKENING

Goddess Energy Secrets & How to Step into Your Divine Power

ANGELA GRACE

© **Copyright 2021 - Ascending Vibrations - All rights reserved.**

The content contained within this book may not be reproduced, duplicated or transmitted without direct written permission from the author or the publisher.

Under no circumstances will any blame or legal responsibility be held against the publisher, or author, for any damages, reparation, or monetary loss due to the information contained within this book, either directly or indirectly.

Legal Notice:

This book is copyright protected. It is only for personal use. You cannot amend, distribute, sell, use, quote or paraphrase any part, or the content within this book, without the consent of the author or publisher.

Disclaimer Notice:

Please note the information contained within this document is for educational and entertainment purposes only. All effort has been executed to present accurate, up to date, reliable, complete information. No warranties of any kind are declared or implied. Readers acknowledge that the author is not engaged in the rendering of legal, financial, medical or professional advice. The content within this book has been derived from various sources. Please consult a licensed professional before attempting any techniques outlined in this book.

By reading this document, the reader agrees that under no circumstances is the author responsible for any losses, direct or indirect, that are incurred as a result of the use of the information contained within this document, including, but not limited to, errors, omissions, or inaccuracies.

CONTENTS

Claim Your bonuses below	v
Preface	xi
Introduction	xv

1. THE HIDDEN DIVINE POWER WITHIN YOU   1
   The Magic of Femininity   3

2. TAPPING INTO YOUR DIVINE ENERGY TO HEAL YOUR SHAME   7
   What Is Feminine Energy and How to Activate It?   9

3. HOW TO STOP GIVING AWAY YOUR DIVINE FEMININE POWER   15
   Clear Your Divine Vessel and Release Negative Energy   17

4. CREATING HEAVEN ON EARTH TOGETHER   21
   Tempted to Tear Others Down?   22

5. YOUR SOUL RETURNING FROM PAST LIFETIMES   27
   Clearing Your Karma from Your Past Life   29

6. LOVE THY SELF, SKYROCKET SEXUALITY, AND POUR OUT INSPIRED CREATIVITY   35
   Open Your Chakras and Love Yourself   38

7. EMBRACING YOUR FEMININITY   43
   Driving Men Wild   46

8. RELEASE PAST TRAUMA AND MAKE SPACE FOR YOUR DIVINE FEMININE AWAKENING   52
   Unburden Yourself from Heavy Baggage   54

9. GRASP YOUR DIVINE FEMININE AWAKENING   59
   Are You Waking up from Your Hibernation?   60

10. GUIDED MEDITATIONS TO TAKE YOU BY THE HAND   65
    Balancing Masculine and Feminine Energies Guided Meditation   66

11. MANIFESTING YOUR BEAUTIFUL LIFE WITH
    YOUR DIVINE FEMININE ENERGY   72
    Law of Attraction and Feminine Energy   74

    Afterword   81
    References   87
    Your Feedback is Valued   91
    Your *bonus* Audiobook is Ready   93

CLAIM YOUR BONUSES BELOW

To help you on your spiritual journey, we've created some free bonuses to help you clear energetic baggage that no longer serves you and manifest a life that suits you better. Bonuses include a companion video course with over 4.5 hours of empowering content, energy-tapping videos, powerful guided meditations, journals, and more.

You can get immediate access by going to the link below or scanning the QR code with your cell phone.

https://bonus.ascendingvibrations.net

Free Bonus #1: The 3-Step Chakra Tune-Up Course

Want to know a unique way to target the chakras? Elevate Your Existence by Targeting the Subconscious, the Physical, & the Spiritual

- Discover a unique 3-step chakra targeting method that so many people aren't taking advantage of!
- Hack your brain, elevate body, mind, and spirit, and release blocks holding you back from greatness
- Awaken amazing energy to tailor a reality that suits you better
- Stop wasting precious time on ineffective methods

Free Bonus #2: The Manifesting Secret Formula Toolkit
Are you done with settling in life, wasting precious time, and ready to attract your highest potential to you?

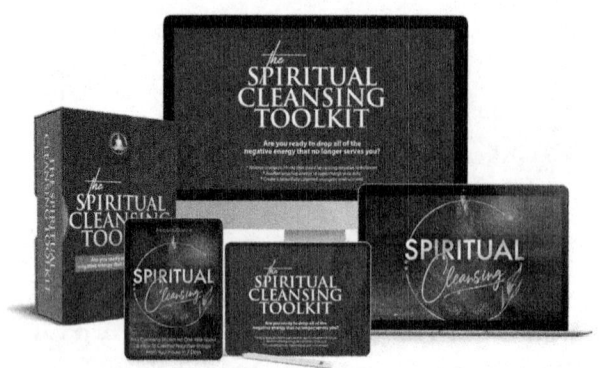

Free Bonus #3: The Spiritual Cleansing Toolkit
Are you ready to drop all of the negative energy that no longer serves you?

- Release energetic blocks that could be causing imbalances
- Awaken amazing energy to supercharge your aura
- Create a beautifully cleansed, energetic environment

Free Bonus #4: A Powerful 10-Minute Energy Healing Guided Meditation

All of these amazing bonuses are 100% free. You don't need to enter any details except for your email address.
To get instant access to your bonuses, go to

https://bonus.ascendingvibrations.net

PREFACE

If you're tired of not being looked at as the goddess that you are, then keep reading. Have you been suppressed for ages and want to step into your power? Are you endlessly giving away your power to other people? Do you often withhold parts of yourself that you wish you could express? Perhaps you judge yourself and feel ashamed. The number one element that will strip you away from your divine magic and power is feeling ashamed. Your life-bearing energy has been suppressed for far too long. It's time to speak your truth.

It is not by chance that you picked up this book, especially before making the big life decision you are thinking about making. Your magic, your wisdom, your life-giving energy may have been covered up and hidden from the world. As women, we all naturally have this magic inside of us, we are creators of the material world, we are the creatrixes.

Are you ready to remember the magic you have inside of you? Are you ready to connect to the self love you need to heal yourself? Women don't just birth children, we birth all of creation into existence. You may have been suppressed for far too long. Just take a look at the society around you. There are so many demeaning places for women, where they are made to feel as though they are nothing or that

PREFACE

their natural, sensual and sacred femininity is something to be ashamed of and used for the benefit of others. Has society conditioned you to suppress and shame the divine sensual part of yourself? You are allowed to tap into that energy again and express yourself how you damn well please.

It is not by chance that you are reading this page. Perhaps you have incarnated into this being to break the paradigm of how society views and shames women. Most of us don't realize the magic and the power that we hold inside our souls. We are all goddesses and our bodies are our sacred temples. Perhaps you are tired of patterns of being a doormat and not moving forward on your path to your authentic self. You may have forgotten your power and that you are a vessel of the divine.

We are ushering in a new world together. By tearing each other down, breaking each other apart, judging and competing with one another, we are suppressing the forthcoming of a new golden age. Come back into the divine feminine cycle of creation. We are supposed to be respected as women and we have to reclaim that power. When you reclaim your power, you stop giving it away to other people. Society has tricked us into giving away our power and not feeling as powerful as we should. We are the rainbow bridge between matter and the spirit world. Tap back into that magic. Reclaim your power.

Here is just a tiny fraction of what you'll discover:

- How to replace or balance masculine traits with feminine traits
- Feminine energy awakening secrets that will appeal to younger and more mature women alike
- Great hints and exercises, a pre-planned morning ritual to follow and the most incredible, life changing trauma release secrets which you can start applying to clear what no longer serves you today.

This book is designed to empower you even if you've never read a spiritual book before, or if you have failed time and time again to awaken your divine feminine energy in the past. This is because there is room for all of us to rise. We must follow the simple and direct path to our awakening. There is no competition between us, we are all one.

So if you want to reclaim your power to heal the world and the wounds that have been caused by us all living in a predominantly masculine society for so long, then read on. This is a book for all women, no matter your age, stage of life, or your situation. Whether you are hoping to find some way of finding peace and balance within yourself or wanting to step into your goddess power. It's time to access new depths of self-love, acceptance, inner strength, clarity, and step into a more complete and empowered relationship with yourself.

INTRODUCTION

Welcome to my book, dear feminine readers! I am so happy to see you landing here, as this means that your instinct and inner power have made you question everything in life. You might have experienced several signs of awakening your divine feminine energy, so you are trying to fill in the gaps and see what lies ahead. There are many other women like you, trying to figure out what to do with that constant urge to discover more about their past, as well as their present and future. By taking part in this awakening, you connect to the universe and find your place in the world. So eventually, you stop wondering about your purpose in life and stop questioning your power.

Have you awakened your divine feminine energy, implementing it in your life? Or, have you ever felt powerless and without a voice, in pursuit of something to support your claims and have your back? Why would you need to depend on others, when you can claim what is yours and receive everything that has been taken from you? Divine feminine energy is what drives women to grandeur. Flowing from within, it expands and releases its uniqueness into the world and the universe. Without it, you feel like you are in hibernation. No one wants to stay like this forever, unable to move and act, reclaiming what they have lost.

INTRODUCTION

In my perception, you are in fact not living your best life, unless you are already healing yourself. This feminine energy which flows from within you can help you heal the wounds and feel reborn. If you are wondering how to elevate your life, how to truly discover what you are made of and claim what has been yours all along, then this awakening of your inner goddess is the best way to go. Until now, you have been missing out for not acting on intuition. There are a plethora of benefits deriving from this awakening process, enabling you to open yourself to the universe and fully perceive the meaning of the world. As a woman, you are a healer. So you need to step up and accept the purpose with which you have been blessed.

It is true that you have been suppressed for years and years on end. As a woman, you have suffered through injustice and you have been stripped of your extraordinary nature. All these elements that have made you exactly who you are, have now been suppressed and you have hidden them deep inside. However, it is time to open your eyes and realize that your identity is to be cherished, rather than persecuted. Patriarchy could not have been more wrong. Women are sacred, and this is how they are supposed to be treated.

AMAZING BENEFITS LIE AHEAD

There are literally endless benefits to harnessing Goddess Energy, so I urge you to continue reading this book. You will discover so much about who you are, what you are meant to do in life, how to cope with challenges, and how to improve your relationships with others and yourself. It will help you to understand the basic terminology, while it

INTRODUCTION

will help you dig deeper within your soul to find the answers you have been looking for. This book is going to show you how to trigger these changes in your life, from the standpoint of a woman who needs to comprehend the universe. Of course, you must keep reading to discover the secrets inside!

If you have experienced shame and fear, you need to awaken your feminine energy. Assuming that you have wasted countless years trying to find out more about your purpose in life, you will see the light at the end of the tunnel. You will eventually find your place in the world, which offers closure and ignites wonderful emotions deep within your soul. If you have been feeling insecure, worthless, not enough to please others and stand by their side, then this book will show you the truth. You are divine. Everyone else should be proud and feel privileged just to be around you.

Find out what this power means to you, how it will affect your life and take you to the highest level of awareness. See through the signs and comprehend the meaning of being a Starseed, a wise soul with thousands of lives and countless incarnations with the sole purpose to help and support others. These entities are so powerful and wise, while at the same time, so blissfully ignorant and filled with hopes and dreams. Discover how you can reach out to other like minded individuals, possibly getting closer to your soul family.

At the same time, in this book you will learn how to avoid wasting your feminine energy. Why do you do that? How can you stop? Read through the tips and experiential advice that comes straight from the heart, so that you will know what to avoid. Your energy is divine and exquisite, so you should not waste it without purpose. You should not throw it away to those who do not appreciate it, feeling drained and unappreciated. Instead, you will learn how to preserve and protect your energy. This is your very essence, after all.

Coming to terms with your sexual awareness is definitely one of the most wonderful benefits you will get from reading this book. Are you feeling disappointed by your sex life? Do you just ignore your desires, sinking in a self loathing that prevents you from truly letting go and surrendering to pure joy? You will find out why it is imperative that you stop suppressing yourself. It is in your power to regain control of

INTRODUCTION

your body and use it as a vessel to feel utter pleasure. No taboos, no second thoughts, no self doubts. Then, letting go of trauma is truly helpful and can offer you some closure. Despite what has happened during childhood, you cannot drown in the same negative thoughts forever. Instead, you need to take matters into your hands and do what is best for you long term. You should encounter your fears, which is exactly what I am going to show you in this book.

Meditations are truly amazing, versatile and uplifting. Don't you know how to practice them? You shouldn't worry, since I have created some cool meditations to cover your needs. Feel free to try them out and see for yourself if they work like a charm—I am positive they will! And finally, after having grasped what feminine energy is all about and how you can ignite it, you will have the chance to attract everything you have been craving for in life. How does that sound?

Discovering My Own Divine Feminine Energy

I was not born knowing about my divine feminine energy, although my gift has always made me wonder if there is something more than what meets the eye in my life. In fact, I had been rejecting my feminine energy, if I look back at the way I lived my life. My career was so demanding and stressful that it made me build a masculine shell to protect myself against the patriarchal society which dominated my professional life. Due to my competitiveness, I had focused on manifesting mainly masculine traits, so that I would become equal to men. This is pretty much what most modern women strive for, isn't that right?

Let me tell you a little bit about myself and my journey. In my life,

INTRODUCTION

I have been blessed with a caring partner and wonderful friends, as well as a beautiful house and a vibrant lifestyle. I have always felt lucky, along with my ability to overcome the hardships and demanding challenges at work. After all, I always delivered and this was something that filled me with pride and satisfaction. However, as time went by and I evolved, I found it hard to stop and appreciate the moment. I was often left hungry for more, always in pursuit of new thrills. Suddenly, what had kept me going that far was not enough.

Even though I came across as strong and powerful, this was not what I really believed about myself. On the contrary, I second guessed pretty much everything I did, every decision I made. My confidence was gone, undermined by my worries that I would be found lacking and ridiculed by others. Just the thought of being outranked at the office filled me with terror. So I tried to figure out what was wrong. I tried to analyze the emotions that emerged out of the blue, spoiling all the hard efforts that I have made to get to the top—or so I thought. Soon, believe it or not, I stumbled upon the magic of her divine feminine energy and it has affected my own life in more ways than I can describe.

I had some breakthroughs, as past memories appeared right in front of my very eyes, leaving me at awe. Although at first I chose denial as my defensive mechanism, I eventually became more aware of what was happening. I felt my inner goddess calling. As I closed my eyes, I would travel to mystical places far away and out of our dimension. I listened to my body and my divine feminine energy, as I evolved into the sacred creature that I am. All my fears and doubts vanished into thin air. It was very hard for me to do that, but I came to accept all the facades of my journey. My journey has brought me here, trying to pass on my hard earned knowledge and wisdom to you.

You should know that I truly appreciate you choosing to read what I have to say. All this information I have gathered here is a result of my yearning to explore my inner self and reach my highest level of awareness. I hope you find your purpose, like I have found mine. And I truly hope we meet again, after you have opened yourself to this new transcendental experience that is going to shift your mindset once and for all. Happy reading and enjoy, everyone!

1
THE HIDDEN DIVINE POWER WITHIN YOU

It is not your fault that you have forgotten what it is like to communicate with your divine feminine. Your inner goddess is not accessible for a reason. Living in a predominantly masculine society for so long has caused patriarchal wounds and covered up the divine feminine power we each have inside of each of us. Our society has negatively conditioned us to believe that female sensuality, natural being, sexuality and expression of oneself is something that should be looked down upon or shamed, when in reality, we are goddesses and SHOULD express ourselves how we please. There is no right or wrong, there is no such thing as restriction and shame, hesitation and doubt, in your book. You are a woman and you are holding the power to rule the world.

Society has tricked us into giving away our power and not feeling as powerful as we should. Women were meant to rule the world, through love and compassion. There are extraordinary elements in feminine energy that make women exceptional leaders, as well as influencers and mentors. A woman can inspire and affect others, guide them through the most challenging situations and provide care, nourishment and unconditional love. These components are unique, ideal for any society. However, things have changed dramatically over the years and now women have been stripped of their own power and uniqueness.

In order to survive, women have been forced to shed their own skin and transform into something that doesn't quite reflect who they really are. Could you ever imagine what a peacock would feel, if they cut down their tail? This would be against their nature, so the peacock would most likely stay shocked for a long time, unable to process what has been done. It is similar to what happens to a woman, once she is deprived of her distinctive traits. She doesn't even recognize herself, since she has associated her very existence with some of these characteristics. Still, over the years, women have survived and have managed to change their standpoint. They have created the foundations to reveal their inner power to the world. And this has not always been easy to accomplish.

Women have learned the hard way that being feminine is not something to take lightly. These components have been fought against for ages, mainly from men who felt threatened by the overwhelming power of women. In combination with their own lack of confidence, men decided to oppose the dominance of the female gender. Women would be persecuted and punished for their very being. It was mayhem, and the repercussions have been mind blowing. It still feels like witch hunting, against those women who have a solid and ambitious vision in their life. Even though we live in a modern society and most stereotypes have vanished into thin air, there are some things that are more resistant to change. Nonetheless, this doesn't mean that we should give up trying.

It is essential to reclaim your power to heal the world and the patriarchal wounds that have been caused by us all living in a predominantly masculine society for so long. This is not going to be easy. It will require time, hard work and patience. But it is inevitable. Justice will be restored, and the rights which have been deprived of females all over the globe will be returned. You deserve to feel powerful and to release that power without any hesitation. It is magical, so you are entitled to that transcendental experience, which will change your life forever.

THE MAGIC OF FEMININITY

When we think of masculinity, we always focus on the end goal. In this way, we are able to measure the results and evaluate masculine behavior. However, with femininity things are quite different. A feminine way of behavior concentrates mainly on the experience. It is far more sensitive and deals with an issue, from the perspective of compassion, creativity and all these fabulous concepts. Unlike masculinity, though, it cannot be measured. So how can you value femininity, when you cannot quantify its results?

For years and years, femininity has been degraded and looked down on, as if it were inferior to masculinity. Most women have been forced to put their feminine traits aside, so that they would become more competitive in the world and seek to which they were entitled. *"This is a man's world"*, right? Instead of letting our guard down and allowing our feelings to take control, we women have felt suppressed for far too long. We have been judged unworthy to what we have been doing, rather than what we were supposed to be. It is a slippery slope here, introducing self-fulfilling prophecy into the mix. According to that socio-psychological phenomenon, an individual is prone to predict certain behavioral patterns and then stick to them, in a form of validating their beliefs (Wikipedia Contributors, 2019).

But why would anyone reject their feminine side? It is part of their inner balance, just like it is represented in the Yin and Yang symbol (Peterson, 2020). Even though the different traits may come across as entirely opposite, in reality they are interdependent and complement one another. This is the concept of dualism, with a perpetual flow balancing each entity. A woman should embrace masculinity, in order to pursue one of her goals. Still, at the same time she should celebrate her femininity. This is what enables her to enjoy things and experiences, even without any apparent gain.

A widespread misconception about femininity is being directly associated with gender. This could not be further from the truth. As discussed above, there are both feminine and masculine components within every single one of us. Nevertheless, in a patriarchal society, the feminine components have been diminished. Their value has been depleted. Instead, masculine traits are what matter the most. When a man focuses on his feminine side, all the world misunderstands him. There is no room for feminine traits, which are considered to be weaknesses. So this misconception has led to women in constant struggle to imitate men and withhold their own power.

Feminine power is irreversible, though. It is unending and includes the entire universe. A feminine is a healer, a nurturer, a caregiver, she creates and supports, she uses empathy and affection. These are elements that should be celebrated, instead of being hunted down and criticized heavily. Women throughout the centuries have contributed to the improvement of the world as we know it, whether or not their contribution has actually been recognized by society. A distinctive example of reality distortion and lack of appreciation when it comes to female contribution is related to Mary Magdalene.

The Example of Mary Magdalene

Are you sure you know the actual story of Mary Magdalene? Or maybe you have been tricked into thinking that she was a prostitute, lacking morality and purpose in life? The truth is that Mary Magdalene was trained under the wings of Isis. She then played an important role in the life of Jesus, teaching him about sexual alchemy and allowing him to overcome boundaries in the physical world. No wonder that she, of all people, is present in His Resurrection! She bears witness to Jesus having risen from the dead to join his Holy Father up in Heaven, and she contributes greatly to the foundation of Christianity.

However, the Church was not very kind to Mary Magdalene. In fact, most people associated her with being a whore, a woman of no value. She was a sinner, according to the Books. Jesus forgave her and showed her the virtuous way of living. But is this really what happened? From our understanding, this is hardly the case. Mary was a powerful woman, who belonged to no one and charted her own course. This is why, unlike most women of her time, you will not see "of X" following her name. Typically, X would be the masculine name, which revealed who the woman belonged to back in the day. Women were the property of men, which pervaded every aspect of their life, including their names. In Mary Magdalene, you will find her origin (being from the famous fishing town of Magdala). She traveled with Jesus, and helped spread his word. Does this sound like a woman of no value?

The Church may have changed her story's facts to suppress women, branding Mary a harlot. Nonetheless, she was a sacred priestess with great power and influence. Mary was independent and guided Jesus, supporting and nurturing him. There is no doubt that Jesus thought highly of her, otherwise she would not be included in his inner circle. Even in the difficult times of pain and suffering, Jesus chose her to remain by his mother's side. This shows just how much he trusted Mary and had faith in her. This theory is in alignment with Dan Brown's novel *The Da Vinci Code* (netage, n.d.). In this case, Mary was depicted as the wife of Jesus Christ.

Moving past myth and religious beliefs, it is safe to assume that Mary was considered dangerous to a patriarchal society. She was strong and did not hesitate to project her power. In fact, she held a special position in the life of a prominent personality—Jesus. Unlike most of the women of her time, she did not compromise her beliefs. Instead, she took a stand and was judged. Maybe the accusations that she was a woman of no honor reflect the profound urge of men to discredit her. Otherwise, a female would replace them and this was something they could not stand.

It is a shame that Mary Magdalene has not received her fair share of universal recognition. More people should know what really happened. More people should be grateful for Mary Magdalene, as she paved the way for other women to stand up and claim their rights. On the contrary, her presence remains ambiguous through the years. It is very difficult for a patriarchal society to admit to having been outranked by a female. Nevertheless, in the philosophy of Jesus, women have always been cherished and their value has never been questioned.

2
TAPPING INTO YOUR DIVINE ENERGY TO HEAL YOUR SHAME

I totally understand why you choose to hold back on your personal self expression because I've been there. Actually, I have been shamed in the past for my sexuality, and for being who I am. My self confidence did not come overnight. It is a work in progress, with its ups and downs, as with every journey. Believing in myself and celebrating my individuality has been my end goal, which I finally reached through awakening my divine energy. Only by realizing that I am unique and amazing and sacred did I get the chance to overcome my fears, and free myself from prejudice and fear.

When I was a teenager, I experienced body shaming. I was rather developed for my age, meaning that my body was quite different from those of other girls. Adolescence can be really cruel for girls, because you see all these radical changes occurring and you can do nothing to stop them. You are in a rollercoaster of emotions, while at the same time your body is changing rapidly. This can be really disappointing, because it prevents you from fitting in and showing the rest of the world that you are like them. You need to belong, but my body made it difficult for that to happen.

Obviously, there was nothing I could do about the changes that took place on my body, other than wear baggy clothes and feel horrible. Instead of finding support among my peers, I found that most classmates would make fun of me and shame me for my body. Interestingly enough, many of them were females. Instead of sticking up for me and accepting me for who I was, they criticized me for no reason and cast me aside. As a result, I eventually started wearing provocative clothes that did not hide my body anymore. On the contrary, I chose outfits that highlighted my curves and revealed that I was sexy and all grown up. Unlike what I believed, this did not have the effects that I would have hoped for. It made my classmates strike even harder, shame me for my self expression and my sexuality. It was a lose-lose situation for me throughout high school.

I spent years trying to come to terms with my body and my own sensuality—until I eventually realized the truth. You see, no one should be judged or looked down on based on what they wear, what they look like, how they behave. Both my former and latter behavior derived from my insecurity and my eagerness to be part of a team. I was innocent and did my best, discovering what I really wanted in life. Being a teen comes with heavy baggage and being shamed only made things worse. It pushed me further from my goal of trying to understand who I am. But my actions were well within my rights, no matter what. It is my body, so I should wear the clothes that make me feel happy and comfortable. It doesn't matter if my breasts are big or small, if I am fat or thin, if my skin is perfect or not. Being shamed took its toll on me, making me an introvert and creating traumas that I have been trying to heal ever since. All that because of shame.

Shame emerges from comparing yourself to your standards and falling short. But where have these standards come from? It is society that dictates what we must do, how we must behave, what we must avoid at all costs. According to society, some behavioral patterns are acceptable, whereas others should be criticized. In order to avoid feeling isolated and left behind, we tend to comply fully with these directives. No matter if we feel like expressing ourselves in a different manner, we end up being exactly the same as everyone else. We do that to avoid embarrassment and social isolation. And these standards are both conscious and subconscious, with the subconscious being even harder to deal with. How can you address a problem, when you don't even know it's there?

Overcoming shame is one of the best things to experience in life. You feel like a huge weight is lifted off your shoulders. Unfortunately, it takes a lot of time for an individual to move past the initial shame and discover how to feel happy again. You do not deserve that burden. You do not deserve to feel like less of a person, just because you are different. Every person is unique and your divine energy is here to remind you of that. Rather than feeling inferior to others, you should really celebrate your difference. This reflects just how wonderful you are, how unique and amazing. To do that, you must get in touch with your feminine energy.

WHAT IS FEMININE ENERGY AND HOW TO ACTIVATE IT?

Many people associate feminine energy with gender. However, this is far from the truth. In fact, an individual is in need of the perfect balance between masculine and feminine traits. When we talk about the masculine energy, we talk about logic and achieving goals. It is more utilitarian, which is great. On the other hand, we refer to feminine energy as the energy creating life. It focuses on beauty, without necessarily being associated with practicality. Both masculine and feminine energy need to be in balance, offering the individual a complete personality to cherish.

Some of the fundamental characteristics of feminine energy are insight, intuition, forgiveness, openness, harmony, sensuality and creativity. You feel the need to indulge in pure enjoyment when doing things in life, rather than evaluate them based on how beneficial they can be to you. Let's think of it this way. When you make yourself a cup of coffee in the morning, why do you do that? If it is because you want to wake up and you know your brain will get stimulated by the aromas of the coffee brewing and the distinctive taste, then you have activated your masculine energy. On the contrary, if you make coffee because you enjoy drinking it, then you are driven by your feminine energy. You know that something sparks joy in your life and you indulge in it, going deeper into the beauty of even the slightest action.

Feminine energy is all about connecting with nature. We are in absolute alignment with the universe, so we need to really listen and connect to nature, rather than go against it. We women are healers, embodying divinity. Feminine energy is nurturing and caring, it holds the formless potential to accomplish everything that we have ever set our minds on. That type of energy moves through life flowing effortlessly, as life is flowing right through our body. It is that precious harmony we all seek in life. You feel it within you, expanding and releasing its power into the world.

It is not easy to activate feminine energy, even if you have fully comprehended its magnitude. The truth is that in a patriarchal society, this very energy has been pushed aside for thousands of years. We have suppressed feminine characteristics, in favor of masculine ones that make us look stronger and invincible. In order to awaken feminine energy, you must become balanced and come to terms with your inner rhythm. You need your inner vibe, the special movement starting from within. An excellent way to achieve that is through drumming. It doesn't matter what kind of drum you use. Just find one that vibrates and offers you the opportunity to tap on it and produce the rhythm that will awaken you.

What you need to do is connect the rhythm you produce with your heartbeat. Just boom, boom, boom while breathing and becoming aware of your own special vibe will give you the opportunity to activate your feminine energy. You will feel it flowing through your veins, surrounding you in a warm and soft manner. Alternatively, you can use activation meditations, such as Shamana drumming. But no matter what you do, make sure you stay relaxed and focus on your breathing. This is one of the basic things you need to do, so as to align your body and soul to the world. Feel your breathing, control it, feel relaxed and listen to your inner rhythm.

Create an inspiring and calming atmosphere. Activating your feminine energy requires time and effort. You need to be comfortable within your surroundings, so as to promote that change to take place. Turn off the lights, because darkness is able to awaken the energy through eliminating distractions. Artificial lights can keep you at a distance, so you should get closer to nature by keeping all your lights turned off. If you are home, you can energize your body by walking back and forth. This creates the vibrations you need. You can light a candle to add some mysticism into the air, be inspired by the soothing fragrances and drive your inner energy to expand. To acquire harmony, try dancing and drumming. This will allow you to feel the rhythm, feel the vibe bursting from within. Listen to that rhythm and go with the flow. You have now connected to your feminine energy, activating it to show you the way. Obviously, the idyllic ambiance in the dark would not be complete without your external connection to the moon. Go out and look at the stars and the moon, taking in the fresh air and relishing absolute calmness all around you. Finally, engage in some stretching to tone your muscles and flex your body. This is your vessel to activate feminine energy and manifest it, so prepare that vessel properly.

Self Esteem Raising Exercises to Implement

You can tap into your divine feminine energy to heal this shame. Restore your self esteem and your lost confidence in a caring and nurturing manner. Your greatest shame and deepest traumas can actually be a blessing in disguise as these painful elements can actually trigger your awakening. With suffering and darkness comes a breakthrough.

It takes time to transform your beliefs and start blooming from within. Change cannot happen overnight. It is true that we have grown up with our own insecurities. And we have a bunch of them. We have been programmed to try and fit in, rather than stand out. This is why we tend to doubt and second guess our value. In our attempt to enjoy feminine energy awakening, we need to reverse the situation. Below, I am going to show you some tools, which will help you unveil your uniqueness. If you add them to your daily routine as parts of your morning ritual, you will notice a huge difference over time.

First of all, you should add affirmations everyday as part of your training to awaken your inner power. Affirmations are sentences we use to train our mind into changing our point of view. So if you have been used to looking down on yourself, this has got to change. Time to see yourself for who you really are. It is important to understand that you should be cherished and appreciated. Before moving forward with your exploration of your inner self, you need to acknowledge several things. You are allowed to fail. This is one of the basic acknowledgments in life. Failure is part of living and maturing. All the important people have failed in the past, prior to gaining recognition and leaving their mark in the world.

Then, it goes without even saying that you should stop seeking validation. Why would you care what other people think of you? This will only make you crave more positive feedback and depend on that. On the contrary, you should learn how to be independent and powerful. There is no one supporting you in your life more than yourself. You need to be your biggest fan, so you needn't listen to anyone else. If you believe that something is right, then go for it. Trust your instinct, trust what you think rather than what others believe.

Judgment and criticism have no room in your life. Which leads us to our next acknowledgment. Stay away from toxic people. These are the people who always frown on you and leave you bitter. People who think of their personal gain only and who act according to their interests. These people take pleasure in bringing you down, reducing your value, and making you feel bad about yourself. They feast on your unhappiness, which is an absolutely horrible thing to do. Well, guess what. These people don't belong in your life, so you should do your best to get rid of them as soon as possible.

Having said that, you can identify the issues that are dragging you down. For instance, you may think you look ugly. You might believe you are not smart enough, tall enough, successful enough. The list is literally endless. After addressing the real issues, you are ready to begin with the affirmations to work on reversing your beliefs. You will say "I am beautiful", "I am successful", "I am wealthy", "I am healthy" and everything else you need to say. At first, you will feel awkward and uncomfortable during the process. However, as you practice, you will see the difference.

Journaling is another excellent tool you can use, so as to spark your feminine energy. Some people believe in the visual representation of things. If you are one of them, then you will find the idea of keeping a journal extremely useful. You don't have to stress about it. Think of it this way. Sometimes, we have so much information in our mind that it is too hard to keep everything inside. You feel overwhelmed by this data which you cannot process adequately since they are flooding your brain. Through the journal, you can express all you want to in writing. This can be quite cathartic. You spike your creative side and build your organizational skills. Plus, you can track your progress and read through your thoughts anytime you feel like it. You open your body and all the information will flow from within. One especially helpful tip, if you don't know where to start, is to write down a letter from yourself to yourself.

Are you friends with your mirror? If not, too bad! There is an amazing exercise that you can do. You simply need a mirror. Although you can use that in the bathroom, it is preferable to use a hand mirror, so as to adjust the angle and proximity. The problem with our life is that we often neglect to look at ourselves in the mirror. I mean really look—don't just take a momentary glance. So you need to take the mirror and bring it really close to your face, almost touching the tip of your nose. Then, stare right within your eyes. Don't do anything else, just look deep inside your eyes. Don't smile, don't laugh, don't get distracted. You might experience awkwardness, which is totally understandable. You are not used to that level of intimacy with yourself. As soon as you are OK with that, start with your affirmations. You will see that this will shock you. Don't get discouraged if you cry the first time you do this. Soon you will get used to it and the results will be astounding—just like you!

Finally, you need to train your mind not to be bothered by life getting in the way. Obviously, you cannot do that. But bear with me for a moment. Why should you get sad over even the tiniest setback? Why be affected by other people's opinions? This is your life and you should live it exactly the way you want to. So practice not giving a damn about what is going on. Do the things which fill you with joy and satisfaction. Meet with people who make you feel good about yourself and support you all the way. Steer clear of everything that brings you down. You are on the path to greatness, don't forget about that.

3
HOW TO STOP GIVING AWAY YOUR DIVINE FEMININE POWER

Our own existence, the entire world around us, is made of infinite energy from above. This energy is neutral and gets contracted, so as to become matter and create the material world we live in. It gets its physical form and is manifested through our thoughts and feelings, reflecting both our masculine and feminine energy. We need to preserve that energy, stop giving it away, to be happy and accomplished in life. However, this is not an easy task. Energy often flows away and is repelled from bodies, whether or not we are actively aware of it.

Whenever we think about something that is bringing us down, we let our divine feminine power and energy escape us. Take a moment to process that. Imagine that you go out and you have too many cocktails, even though you had convinced yourself that you would limit your alcohol intake to a couple of drinks. You get back home and you start beating yourself up. Thoughts of worthlessness run through your mind, making you feel bad about yourself. You are disappointed and you feel like you are never going to recover from that negative emotion. This is all draining you off your energy. All this self loathing does nothing but keep you diverted from your goals.

The same thing happens with every single thought that you have that brings you down. There are quite a few issues you are dealing with, which can make you feel bad and even lead to depression. If you are unhappy about your finances, if you are let down by your lack of discipline in following a new diet and exercise regime, if you are drawn to the wrong men—all these things drain precious energy. So you need to stop and find ways to protect your feminine energy. You need to prepare yourself to overcome those leaks and hold on to as much energy as possible.

Social anxiety adds to the mix. When you feel uncomfortable and insecure within society, you spend too much energy. Rather than feeling cool and secure in what you are doing, you waste your energy and become exhausted thinking about the consequences. You overanalyze things, you measure the pros and cons, you play scenarios within your head. This is not working out for you. So it is time to break free from this vicious cycle, which has to do with society's opinion about yourself and your value.

As you can imagine, preserving your feminine energy is quintessential for your well being. If you waste that precious energy, it is like you are throwing away your past. All the time spent creating that energy, all the sacrifices that other women have made and that they have suffered, so that you could enjoy the benefits of connecting to your inner goddess, all that would have gone to waste. Are you thinking of denying the very core of your existence? Unless you are on the brink of letting go of your feminine aspect in life, you need to do your best to avoid that. To maintain your divine power, you must treat it with respect and prudence. Do not spend it on thoughts, beliefs, acts, and relationships that do not live up to your standards. If you do, sooner or later you will feel the negative consequences as your energy is running right through you.

CLEAR YOUR DIVINE VESSEL AND RELEASE NEGATIVE ENERGY

There are many different types of people who are wrong for you. They suck you dry and leave you without the tiniest bit of energy. These are the people you don't want in your life, even if at first sight you may think that you do. It is important that you use your feminine energy to protect yourself against narcissists, bad relationship partners, energy vampires, society's judgment and criticism. In this way, you will master the art of preserving your energy and feeling exactly like you are meant to feel—awesome. Detoxification will cleanse your life of unhealthy relationships.

In order for you to clear your divine vessel and release all that negative energy that has been piling up for so long, you need to follow some easy and helpful steps. First off, you must admit that there is too much going on in your life and you are allowing too many people to control you. Does that sound familiar? Why would you ever want to leave the important decisions to others? There is no one who knows what you need better than you. Make sure that you identify these people, who have been sucking the air out of your lungs and remove them from your life.

Set your boundaries so as to avoid wasting your energy. These people will never stop. They will keep on demanding from you as if you are obliged to deliver. What you do and how you live should not concern them. It is not for them to judge and advise you. Nor should they have the power to make your decisions. You are the one in control. It is time to step up onto that pedestal and see the world from a privileged point of view. Then, it is equally important to be selfish and to act in your best interest. Selfishness is not always a bad thing. I am not talking about harming others. Of course not. However, you need to put yourself first and act according to your beliefs, your desires, and your needs. Who else would you want to please? Feel free to pamper yourself, nourish and nurture your body and soul. The happiness you get out of the whole experience is beyond comparison. Plus, it helps you to maintain your feminine energy.

Finally, you need to stop feeling guilty. Guilt is often used to pressure us to act against our will. For example, if you don't want to hang out with a guy, why not confront him and tell him about it? There is no reason for you to prolong the inevitable. In fact, you will be better off without each other, since there is no actual chemistry between you. The same happens when you attend a party that you don't want to, eat food you despise, watch a movie you don't enjoy, and the list goes on and on. Don't apologize for your choices in life. Stand by them and support your decisions. When you apologize, you are contracting your energy. You are pushing it downward, and you feel the pressure. You don't deserve that kind of pressure, so let it go.

When you think about something for too long, you spend energy. For instance, do you recall how many times you longed for love to come along? All this energy is contracted, and you feel tight and suppressed. As a result, you repel what you are looking forward to experiencing—because of that energy contraction. Every time you feel judged or shamed by what you have done, you act in the opposite way from how you would want to act. You are not attracting the things to which you are entitled; you are pushing them away.

So the solution is to release the contraction, by breathing them out and aligning your energy with a higher energy. You get connected to the source energy, since you are more relaxed and you release the tension and the contracted energy flows from within you. There is infinite potential for you out there, as long as you stop limiting yourself. Step out of the consciousness that is not working anymore. Detox your mind and body, by letting go of that suppressed energy.

Activate The Goddess Within

Having released your negative energy, you can now purify your aura to make room for your feminine energy awakening. Are you intrigued to ignite the divine feminine energy from deep inside? Are you ready to activate your goddess from within? You need to put those feminine energy affirmations in your morning ritual, so that you reverse your training and allow your mind to contemplate what you really want to pursue in life. There are several things you should focus on to boost your self awareness and empower your inner divine energy.

You are a goddess and you should start behaving like one. Believe in your power and feel all those positive things that derive from being such a woman. Why are you happy being a female? What makes your heart beat faster? Why would others go out of their way to come a little closer to you? If you think you are not worthy, you need to reconsider. People have gone to extremes because they wanted to do something that they felt motivated to accomplish. They have stayed out in the cold, in really bad weather conditions, risking their life and abstaining from food and water, because they wanted to reach a high mountain top. Others have fought to the death for a beautiful woman, or to defend their family's honor. There is nothing to prevent someone from coming closer to you, even if this means that they would have to sacrifice something to do so.

Are you still undecided as to whether or not you deserve to communicate with your inner goddess? Really, there should be no doubt. However, when you practice the following affirmation, you will come to open your eyes slowly, and truly see what it means to be you. It is much more than a word or two. It is much more than a feeling or two. You are a reflection of the entire universe, living in perfect harmony. You have come to earth to help mankind and to make the world a better place in so many ways. Everything you do has been blessed. Hence, you don't have to justify your actions or ask for anyone's permissions.

First of all, you should remind yourself of your best qualities. "I am loving", "I am self sufficient", "I am a caring person", "I am kind", and "I am loveable" can all serve as an introduction. "I exude love and compassion", "My spiritual energy is high" and "I am a powerful, self accomplished woman" are equally helpful. You need to be able and let down your guard and surrender to the harmony of nature. It is imperative that you relax and open your soul, so as to receive these affirmations and accept their truthfulness. "I am a queen", "I embody my divine energy", "I am in perfect alignment with my ancient power and wisdom"—these are all excellent affirmations to go on with. "I am the force of the wind", "I am an extension of cosmic creation", "I embrace my sensual energy" and "I express myself truthfully, honestly and without haste" are also amazing affirmations to use.

Through these affirmations, you must open your mind and allow your body to receive all the precious gifts it is about to receive. Your inner goddess waits to be released to the cosmos, so you need to prove yourself worthy of receiving that special honor. You must align with the universe and believe in yourself. Without this alignment, you are doomed to keep your goddess hidden and suppressed for all eternity. Believe in the fact that you are extraordinary and pass this on to your subconscious. "My energy is strong and vital", "I am the young, the new, the ancient and the old", "I am a wonderful manifestation of the Divine Feminine"—these affirmations will keep you on track, even when you fall off the wagon and are set astray.

4
CREATING HEAVEN ON EARTH TOGETHER

Being a woman is a true blessing and it should be considered as such. Over the years, though, women have been shamed and diminished. We have been looked down on for so long that it has nearly become second nature to us. It seems that we are constantly fighting against all odds. In a patriarchal society, being a woman comes with its downside. Nobody is willing to give up on their long-lasting rights. So it is a neverending struggle to prove your worth and earn your place in the world.

This is why we need to stick together. It is us against the world, trying to establish our position in society. Otherwise, we will always be looking over our shoulder, on edge that something is going to creep up behind us and deprive us of whatever we have achieved so far. Isn't that right? We need to make a pledge to help each other and boost our power together. It is our time to rise. As long as we empower one another, we are going to usher in a new golden age which will create heaven on earth where we all can thrive.

Unfortunately, we women have learned the hard way how difficult it is to trust others. Having experienced injustice, you cannot help but remain skeptical all the time. Betrayal is not an unknown world, and it hurts to put yourself out there, exposed to the same threats over and over again. So we have built ourselves a wall, big enough to keep everyone at bay. This can be a great strategy, but it comes with risks. One of the risks that you take is that you may be warding off who can help you. So in your effort to protect yourself (which is absolutely understandable and kudos for that), your wall prevents you from connecting with other women.

However, it is crucial to understand there are more things connecting than dividing us women. Although we come in different shapes and sizes, although we may be miles apart, although our backgrounds vary greatly, it is that special feminine sparkle which brings us together. We are women, meaning that we have achieved greatness through difficult times. This is what defines us. Hardships we have overcome only make us stronger. But they often make us colder towards our own kind. You should not fall for that trap, as it drives you further away from your true essence.

No longer should we tear each other down and judge each other. We are all sacred feminines and we need to start coming together, to remind each other of the magic that we hold inside. When we come together, our energy amplifies and we can send that out to the world to create change. United we stand, divided we fall. It is inevitable that the power comes in numbers. So join a growing network of women and multiply your strength, rather than trying to cause harm.

We are special, you need to wrap your mind around this. The world should be welcoming towards our uniqueness, acknowledging what we are capable of. Nevertheless, reality is much harder. There are obstacles that keep bringing us down. Men seem to have placed us in cages in an attempt to restrain us. Can you imagine what would happen if we were to join forces for the common good? These restraints would be no more. This is our calling, so don't turn your back on it, just because you think that you are better off on your own. You aren't, trust me.

TEMPTED TO TEAR OTHERS DOWN?

There are many people who feel they are obliged to compare themselves to others. When that comparison falls short, there is no other way but to try to diminish the value of the individual who has been proven superior. Does this behavioral pattern seem familiar to you? Are you constantly antagonizing other women? This is not healthy since it prevents you from truly blossoming from within. Instead, you need to focus on your own self, trying to improve and move forward. By wasting your time observing what other people do, you deprive yourself of valuable time spent in personal growth. All these distractions will take their toll on you and leave their scars for good. They will keep you from your true goal and bruise your relationship with your allies.

To be honest, this urge to come across as superior to others might reveal a hard truth for yourself. Perhaps you have been wounded deeply and you now feel compelled to prove your value to yourself and others. Maybe you have not found the recognition that you deserve, and this is something you need to acknowledge before you can resolve it. So the next time that you are about to gossip or judge another person, especially a woman with whom you share many common things, ask yourself this question: what is driving you to behave like this? Is it family, is it your peers who are always judging you for who you are, what you wear, what you do in your life?

If you are tearing down someone else, judging them, or competing with them, then that means you are doing that to yourself. This is a reflection of your own negative emotions. Are you having doubts as to your competence about something? Are you feeling less worthy than what you would have hoped? These doubts might remain subconscious, but they still affect your behavior and spike your insecurity. If you were independent and confident, then you would not spend your time figuring out what others do. You would be too busy trying to perfect your own skills, your performance, your style. This is what you need to aim for. Improve yourself, by figuring out how to stop criticizing others.

So every time you are passing judgment on a female colleague or a friend, a mere acquaintance or a total stranger, try to interpret the signs. Read in between the lines and see what these actions mean. Do you want to be bad towards others? I know this is not the case for you, as a Starseed is never driven by evil. Does that make you feel happy or satisfied in any way? I am sure it doesn't. In fact, it most likely fills you with regret. These actions are clearly not your style. They are most likely a reflection of what you need to heal inside yourself. When you don't like what another woman is doing or don't agree with them, it triggers something inside you that you need to heal.

It is time to unleash your passion and let it guide you, while listening to what your heart dictates. This is the only way for you to start observing things that you have never paid attention to before. There is beauty in the world and in every single one of us. There are infinite ways, in which each of us can live our own lives. In a similar pattern, there are infinite paths we can choose, according to our individual preferences. No right or wrong here, no "one-size-fits-all" solution. It doesn't matter the tiniest bit whether you agree with it or not. You just let everyone be, like they let you—no judgment, no negative vibe, no worries, just pure bliss.

Finding Your Soul Family and Other Starseeds

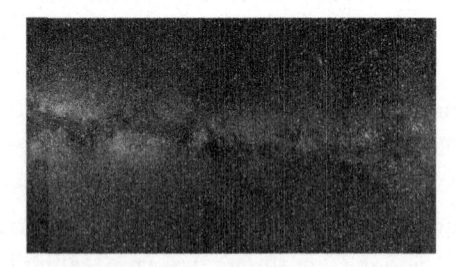

Do you feel like you don't belong here on earth? Have you ever had a near-death experience or have you ever remembered things that you should not have been able to? Then you are probably experiencing what each Starseed goes through during the unveiling of their true essence. A Starseed is an advanced soul who has arrived on earth from other planets and other dimensions. Your purpose is to help humanity in this difficult time of Ascension in which we are living in. I am sure that explains a lot about your life.

Always drawn by the mysteries of life, science fiction, and space, you are sensitive and empathize with other people's feelings. Most would describe you as a dreamer, probably too aloof at times, and an extrovert, with a yearning to help others. This is your calling, after all. You have decided to visit earth, which shows how caring and affectionate you are. You believe in the highest principles, such as love and solidarity, equality and unconditional help.

However, your transition into a human being came at a substantial cost. The cost was none other than oblivion. You forgot your purpose in life, which made you unaware of the challenges you are about to face. Over time, memories come up and you start connecting the dots. It is like a puzzle and you are meant to find the pieces one by one. Although it can feel exhausting, with every new discovery you get a little closer to your end goal. You get closer to finding out more about your calling, about the real reason why you are here now.

I know that, for a Starseed, it can be really lonely here on earth. You feel misplaced, as if you don't have a place to call home. Above all that, you cannot quite communicate with those around you. No one gets you, not even when they pretend that they do. Wouldn't it be nice to surround yourself with like-minded, awakening beings? People you can share everything with and truly connect to—these are the people that will be your soul family. They are so hard to find, but they will eventually find you or you will find them. The powers drawing you close together are much higher than any obstacles that stand in the way.

Of course, there are no ads you can post to meet other Starseeds and awakened creatures. I wish it were that easy! The truth is that you don't even feel 100% sure that you are a Starseed. You have seen the signs, so you know something is up. You are not like others. But are there others like you? The good thing is that you'll know right away. As soon as you meet another Starseed, you will feel as if you have known each other an entire lifetime. Your instinct will be right, as you have been companions from a different dimension.

Starseeds will most likely have the same interests as you. They will be drawn by space and extraterrestrial life, they will enjoy flying and they will be very sensitive. You will identify your own traits in them. You can improve your social life and intensify your awakening by reaching out to these wonderful people. In fact, you will see that your power becomes much stronger when you are around them. Remember that you have the same positive effect on them, too.

Check out seminars and events relevant with spiritualism. Forums and chat rooms, groups on Facebook and websites can help you out. Attending reading or acting classes, meditation and yoga sessions might also work. A planetarium or a place where you can observe the stars are also amazing places to find other Starseeds. Look for that unique vibe in the air, where you feel like you have found the missing pieces. It is a warm and cozy feeling, a sense of accomplishment. Better yet, you will feel the same thing and share your excitement.

5

YOUR SOUL RETURNING FROM PAST LIFETIMES

Through incarnation, we have all been through past lives. We are all in this perpetual journey towards divinity. We choose to come to life as women and the reason for doing so is to get ready for this shift in consciousness. We wish to reconnect with the magic and power with which we have lost touch. Perhaps in a past or parallel life you were executed or condemned for speaking your truth or being a natural healer. You have come back NOW because you can't be killed for this and you can't be silenced anymore.

We came here to remind other women and everyone in the world that we are here to rise and balance out the divine masculine and feminine energies once again, to reclaim our power and heal the world and the patriarchal wounds that have been caused by us all living in a predominantly masculine society for so long. You have come back incarnated in this form ready for the divine feminine energy awakening.

Can you imagine that there was a time when people would hunt us down and kill us, condemning us to a painful death? This would not happen because we had murdered or raped or tortured another human being. Women were only persecuted because men have accused them of witchcraft. Yes, our sacred feminine consciousness due to the inherent ancient connection to the divine feminine has cost us dearly. People burnt us because we were considered evil.

What is evil about holding the power to reach the divine? We were supposed to be protected, worshiped even, because of our connection to divinity. Instead, society wanted to banish us. They would not stop until they had wiped us all clean from the earth. It was a truly bloody persecution, since they would not show any mercy. It was as if they felt threatened by our unique nature. So instead of trying to understand us, they chose to fight. They didn't want to be stripped of their power, and we would prove ourselves worthy of taking up even the greatest challenge.

Fortunately, we have found a way back to claim what is ours. Although we have been persecuted and completely misunderstood throughout history, we have always bounced back, stronger than ever. Throughout history, you will often come across the organized crimes committed against women. Without the tiniest effort to validate the accusations designed to destroy us, men kept on beating. And we kept on taking the punches, getting ready to strike back harder.

Now, our time has come. We need to reverse the current situation and take back what has clearly been stripped from us. We are divine, we are chosen, we are entitled to power and bliss. Why have we waited for so long? It takes time for the wheel to turn. Change cannot happen overnight. We have been waiting patiently, using incarnation to take a female form to claim our rights. And now it is finally time to reap the benefits of our long lasting anticipation.

Are you ready to gain a consciousness of your past lives? Do you feel the urge to truly comprehend what it means to be YOU? If so, you can move forward to the next step. You will be expected to cleanse your inner soul before you delve into the treasures of your past existence. Prior to knowing what has happened to you, it is crucial that you pave the way carefully. Clear your karma from your past lives and prepare yourself to move forward. It is your time to shine, so don't let anything hold you back and drown you in negativity.

CLEARING YOUR KARMA FROM YOUR PAST LIFE

Take a moment to think about a project you have been working on for years. Unless you have set proper foundations, you will soon realize that your entire endeavor might crumble into pieces. It is only fair to assume that you need to be careful when structuring the whole thing. Otherwise, it will probably be a lost cause. Now consider having spent a significant amount of time, only to discover that you have been laboring under an illusion. This can be devastating, to say the least.

The same applies in real life. You cannot expect to move forward unless you have successfully dealt with your past life issues. Anything that has been dragging you down, anything that has been left unresolved, is a ticking time bomb. It may not explode right away, but it will go off eventually. So you should act beforehand and make sure that you have no weights pulling you under. You must be set free from all these issues from your past. This is the only way that you can ever expect to succeed in reaching your divine power.

When you are holding a grudge, you are injuring your karma in a serious way. In a similar pattern, bitterness can hurt you emotionally and prevent you from reaching your divinity. Even though it might sound tempting, you need to steer clear of wishing others ill as they make their way through their life. This is not who you are. Furthermore, you should be grateful for whatever happens. This includes not only the good things, but also the hardships you get through. If something positive comes your way, you are free to enjoy and cherish these moments. On the other hand, when something negative comes your way, be grateful for the challenge. It is a great opportunity to allow you to grow and become more mature.

Negative thoughts are horrible, because they poison you from within. They don't allow you to experience euphoria and relax. Instead, they surround you with unwanted energy. This is not something that you need in your life, so don't invite that energy over. The best thing you can do is let go of negativity. Focus on positive thoughts, optimism and, when in doubt, make a list of all the good things you have in your life. I am sure that they will outweigh the bad things, so you will see the light at the end of the tunnel.

Karma has to do with the actions and reactions that choices bring in your life. If you have been treating others like garbage, you cannot expect the universe to treat you differently. So in order to clear your karma, it is best to filter your behavior and evaluate it accordingly. Be nice to people, smile and treat them with respect. Being loving and caring is never out of fashion. In this way, you will get rid of all the clutter that you are dealing with emotionally and spiritually.

Finally, I cannot stress enough the importance of forgiving others. Sometimes, it is hard to do that. There are behaviors you cannot ignore. People can be very hard and cruel. But vengeance will only make things worse. You will keep on feeling bitter inside since you will never get closure. On the contrary, you will repeat the same scenario all over again, thinking of what has driven you to feel that way. You do not deserve to be stuck in that position. So get over it, forgive, and get rid of what has been burdening you.

Now that you have cleansed the past, it is time to dive deep into our past lives. A wonderful way to do that is through Past Life Regression Therapy. This can work wonders for you, assuming that you have fully comprehended what you are made of. In other words, you need to have completed clearing your karma and, of course, you must have come to terms with being a Starseed. Are you excited? I know I am. Let's move on to the next step, shall we?

Past Life Regression

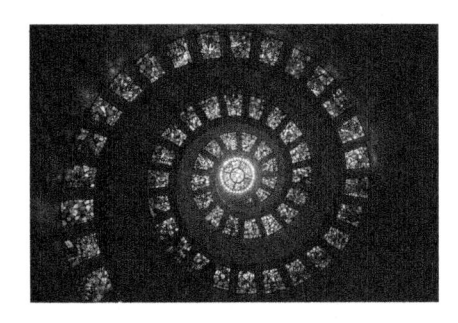

Past Life Regression will guide you towards discovering hidden secrets about your past lives. You have had thousands of them, so it is only fair that you learn more about how you have lived throughout eternity. However, you cannot simply ask and receive. The process is a little more complicated. First, you need to clear your mind completely. Before you get this shift of consciousness, you must make sure that the conditions are ideal. You don't want any distractions interrupting you from your anticipated journey, do you?

Pick a place where you feel comfortable. This will most likely be your home, but you can select another place, if you prefer. Then, wear something that you hardly notice. Cozy pyjamas, a T-shirt and yoga pants or leggings are fine. Just remember that you should clear your mind from any distractions, including those coming from your surrounding environment. Feel the temperature in the room you have selected. Is it too cold or too hot? Are there any bad smells that can set you off course during your session?

After having created the perfect atmosphere, you will need to sit down comfortably and close your eyes. If you want, you can have some relaxing music in the background, as well as lightly scented candles or sticks. It is important to be alone with your thoughts. Now keep your eyes closed and get rid of the tension. Dispose of any thoughts that have been troubling you. Now is your time to concentrate on your breathing and your breathing alone. Each time you inhale, think of the lotus flower. Every time you exhale, that lotus flower opens up and reveals its true beauty.

Slowly but steadily, you will notice that your breathing becomes deeper. You feel that and nothing else. You have become conscious of your existence, appreciating the moment and living only for that. It is time to let go and ascend far away. Are you ready for that journey? Flying is fun, especially when you leave your body and lift higher above the ground through your light soul. You distance yourself from gravity and absorb everything all around you. It is a sight for sore eyes traveling to a different dimension.

Once you reach your destination, you should choose which past life you are going to delve into. There are doors leading to your past lives, which is why you should select which one to open. As mentioned above, you have been through multiple different lives. Not all of them have been equally important, for sure. Evaluate your needs and preferences, figuring out where you want to go. As soon as you reach your decision, set out to descend back to earth. Observe once more what is going on around you, taking in every single detail. Can you see where you are heading? This is very exciting.

Upon arrival to your past life timeline, you will experience your birth. Do not be afraid of the emotions you are about to feel. They will be intense, but you should cherish them. Try to hold on to these memories, as to what it felt like being born. Was it painful, or was it relaxing and blissful? No matter what, keep your eyes open and observe the details. Are your parents with you? Where are you? In which part of the world are you? Before you know it, your life will be passing you by quickly. Flashcards of the most significant things that happened in your life will be displayed before you and you will need to connect the dots.

Were you a good person? Were you healthy? These are just a few of the questions that you will need to answer throughout your journey. According to your past, you will regain memories that will help you out in your present and future life. This is invaluable information that you would not be able to obtain elsewhere. So gather as many details as possible and try to realize if you were worthy of remembering. The odds are that a Starseed is stellar.

At the big finale, you will need to relive your death. This can be a painful experience, but it is imperative that you don't shy away from the experience. Try to figure out if you had a smooth passing, if you were of age, if you had your loved ones beside you. These are truly precious pieces of information as they have left their imprint deep inside you, even though you may not be able to recall the details. You are looking at your life from a higher perspective. The more you know about who you were, the better. It might seem like you are suffocating, but you will be alright in the end. Good as new, with all the valuable lessons that you have learned along the way.

Now, once you have completed this cycle of wandering through your past life, you will be requested to come back. You cannot stay there forever, since you have already experienced everything within that lifetime. The only thing you can do is use that knowledge to your advantage, becoming even wiser and more mature than before. It is that wisdom that will stay with you from now on, assisting you in your struggle to reach out to your divine nature. You are slowly waking up, embracing your feminine side, and moving on to the next step of awareness.

After having wrapped up the journey, you will ascend once more far away in different dimensions and then you will start your descent to your current life on earth. Enjoy the ride and try to hold on to what you have unveiled throughout this experience. When you open your eyes after the past life regression has ended, you will probably feel shocked. You will feel overwhelmed by your recently acquired knowledge. It is certain that you cannot have anticipated all that. Maybe you never would have expected to have been incarnated as a male figure in the past. Perhaps you had never imagined you would be an artist, a philosopher, a housewife, a carpenter.

First, you ought to deal with the shock and come to terms with whoever you have been in your past life. Then, check out your past behaviors. There are patterns that may interpret your ongoing habits. What would you think about scars that have remained intact with every incarnation of yours? Unresolved issues that pretty much define who you are and how you react. These issues have to be encountered, otherwise they will continue to haunt you. This is why it is so crucial to gather information from your past lives, so that you are able to confront these challenges now. Reprogram yourself and enhance your awareness, gaining more wisdom and finding the resources required to elevate your existence.

The more knowledgeable you get through past life wisdom, the more powerful you become and the more you are able to rise above the challenges that you are bound to face in this life. Live up to your expectations, soar, and show what you are truly made of. You are divine, so don't let anyone tell you otherwise. First and foremost, you must love yourself and believe in your power. If you don't, who will?

6

LOVE THY SELF, SKYROCKET SEXUALITY, AND POUR OUT INSPIRED CREATIVITY

Have you been suppressing your feelings for your entire lifetime? Your wounds as a child may have stemmed from other past lives, or they may have resulted from years and years of abuse. This is perfectly understandable, since no one can do something about their past. Children are powerless, fragile and easy to shape. Adults are meant to shield and protect them. However, this is not always the case. Some families are responsible for creating deep wounds that never seem to heal. Children grow up thinking that they are worthless, and that they deserve nothing good in their life.

Traumatized children are on their way to becoming traumatized adults. Endless complexes, feelings of inferiority, and negative thoughts flood their mind. Nevertheless, there is a huge difference between childhood and adulthood. The former comes with an a priori sense of powerlessness. The latter, though, should not be the same. You are a grown up person, capable of making your own decisions. You have the power that it takes to stop that vicious cycle and claim what you are entitled to. There is no room for self pity. Why would you feel sorry for yourself? If something doesn't suit you, change it.

When it comes to emotional stability, old wounds can be very dramatic. They come across as too hard to overcome, drowning you in negativity. As a result, you do not believe in your value and you remain entirely dependent on what others think of you. In the past, it was your father who accused you of being stupid. It was your mother who never showed you affection. It was your classmates who called you names and bullied you. Now who has taken their place? Who is bullying you now?

Self loathing is not for you. You are not the victim here. Even though you may have experienced some negative things in the past, you are fully capable of reversing the situation. Do you believe that you are unworthy? This is something that you need to work on. Otherwise, history will repeat itself and you will find that you are living the same thing over and over again. Take a stand for yourself, take a stand against harassment and honor what you represent. This is your moment, don't forget that.

Being a woman, you understand the feelings you are experiencing, and you are expected to face them. You must release them, so as not to allow them to harm you anymore. No matter how cruel these feelings are, no matter how much pain they put you through, you need to rise up. The only solution to get rid of these negative emotions is to acknowledge them. If you continue to suppress and shove them deep within your soul, you will never feel whole. You will always be lacking something. Dealing with your emotions is quintessential for your well being and understanding of your true value. These emotions are often dark and cold, but still you need to address them, process them and eventually eliminate them.

People who are responsible for your feeling of worthlessness do not belong in your life. Set boundaries and do not fall for the oldest trick in the book. Do not let others determine who you are. Instead, show the world what you stand for and this will be reflected on others. The rest of the world will see you for who you are, paving the way you want them to walk. As you can see, you hold the keys to your freedom, or your captivity. You hold the keys to your happiness, or your misery.

When it comes to romantic relationships, things can get ugly pretty fast. A toxic relationship can poison you, which is something you definitely do not deserve. Why put up with this kind of behavior?

If your significant other doesn't live up to your standards, then you should think twice before letting them occupy such a precious spot in your life. Being your loved one is an honor and he should thank you for that. It is not your place to beg, nor is it to offer one opportunity after the other. A couple must be in perfect alignment with each other, allowing both to blossom and become better. What you need from your relationship is reassurement, safety and love, respect and affection. Does he tick those boxes for you or not?

Assuming that you are having doubts as to the quality of your relationship, you already hold the answer in your hands. Get out of this toxic relationship, before it gets worse. You should feel sure when you are with him, not prolong your insecurity. A man who wants to be in your life will show you with every opportunity he gets, not add to your negative thoughts and fears. Don't settle for anything less than what you are entitled to. You deserve so much and you should not stop until you find that.

Before you know it, you will find your true purpose in life and you will not even recall what the past had brought you. There are people who make a difference and those who come into your life just to prove we are not all the same. Guess who you should aim at introducing in your life! In this book, you will find all the help you need, so as to consider what your passions are and how you can incorporate those into your life. Which are the things that inspire you the most? What do you enjoy doing? You can find intriguing activities, pursue your dreams or experiment with different things in your daily routine. Sooner or later, your passions will emerge.

This is the only way to achieve that healthy balance in your life. Unless you reach the point of self love, you cannot have high hopes. On the contrary, you will compromise and avoid reaching true greatness. All these barriers that appear in the shape of inadequate people will continue taking their toll on you. Are you willing to let them gain control over your life? I don't think so. You are meant for reaching your divinity. So how can you settle for less than that? It is all out there for the taking. You just need to reach out and grab what you want. This will be the beginning of amazing things happening to you.

Once you have found your balance, you will reveal a whole new world of potential. You will get the opportunity to activate, enhance, and skyrocket your sexuality and creativity. You will feel like a whole new different person, ready to take on the world. When you find someone to share this new world with, you will have acquired all the tools you need for making the most out of your relationship. You will no longer be filled with fear or guilt. Contrary to what you may believe about yourself now, you will have clarified that you are awesome and you deserve the whole wide world. All that comes from the inspired process of opening your chakras.

OPEN YOUR CHAKRAS AND LOVE YOURSELF

Are you ready to love yourself? I know, it can be hard at times. Still, remember that you are unique. Think of your journey, all those past lives joined together. This concentrated wisdom deriving from countless lives has become your hard earned possession. You are equipped to face life with confidence, self love and appreciation. Your companion will join you, in an adventure you will both treasure. There is no room for looking back, there is no place for self loathing and endless doubts getting in the way of your happiness.

Open your chakras, so that you enjoy your relationship to the fullest. There are seven chakras you will need to open from your body, improving your energy flow and seeing the benefits in your connection with your significant other. Don't hold back on your sexual pleasure, don't be afraid of releasing that power. You will find that unlocking those parts of your body will help you achieve sexual divinity, gaining control over every inch of your body in a magical, almost transcendental manner.

The first chakra is the root, at the end of your backbone. This signifies the level of trust cultivated between you and your partner. You cannot be with a person you don't trust, can you? Indulge in aromatherapy and burn Muladhara incense, as well as essential oils. Sandalwood, ginger, cypress are all great for that. Repeat affirmations that bring positive effects about safety, in order to develop that sense of security all around you and pass it on to your relationship. "I am safe", "I am not afraid", "The universe will protect me", "I love my body and myself" are just a few of the affirmations you can use, as many times as you feel like it. Practice yoga and focus on postures like the warrior, squad, mountain, or goddess.

The second chakra is sacral, which is all about acceptance. In this case, you will need Svadhisthana incense and essential oils to burn. Chamomile, patchouli, rose are all splendid options. Now you must repeat affirmations, which are relevant to your sensual and creative nature. "I embrace change", "I deserve to experience sexual pleasure and fun", "I feel comfortable in my body" will work amazingly for you. Bound angle and happy baby are the best yoga postures for healing your sacral chakra.

Moving on to your third chakra, which is the solar one and signifies appreciation. This is another crucial element in a relationship. Manipura incense and essential oils are in order here, so choose among cinnamon, musk and saffron. You must repeat affirmations about your own personal power. "I am ambitious", "I am capable of taking on any challenge" and "I will make positive changes in my life" will all help you unblock this chakra. As for yoga postures, go for sun salutations, the warrior posture and the boat.

Obviously, the fourth chakra is one of the fundamentals in love. It is the heart chakra, having to do with the purity of love and affection experienced in the relationship. Orange, jasmine, lavender are all inspiring aromas which work really well for you, since you should burn Anahata incense and essential oils. Affirmations unblocking your heart include "I am open to love", "I love myself and I love all other people" and "I forgive myself and others". Yoga will help you direct your heart towards the sky, so the perfect postures for that are camel, bridge and dog facing upward.

Throat is the fifth chakra, showing positive expression and admiration. A couple should support one another and express their thoughts, respect, and love in a way that heals the soul. Sage, peppermint, and eucalyptus are perfect for burning Vishuddha incense and essential oils. Through affirmations, you should focus on openness in communication. Try "I communicate honestly", "I listen actively" and "I believe in authenticity when communicating". The fish pose, camel, and plow are great yoga postures for you to try out, so as to concentrate on your throat and thyroid.

The third eye chakra is the sixth in line, representing harmony. A relationship should be built on harmony, otherwise it cannot last long. To unblock that chakra, you must burn Ajna incense and essential oils. Myrrh, nutmeg, and St. John's Wort are superb. Your affirmations should be all about awareness and trusting your intuition, opening your third eye. "I let my intuition guide me", "I trust in what I feel" and "My spiritual truth guides me" are all spot on. Dolphin, locust and child's pose will help you greatly in your goal to reach that higher level of awareness in yoga.

Finally, the crown. This chakra represents connection, which is the quintessence of a relationship. Stay connected and build a wall around you, so that you feel safe and intimate with each other. Burn Sahaswara incense and essential oils, such as frankincense, myrrh and camphor. Your affirmations here should be relevant to enlightenment and deep, spiritual connection with yourself and others. "I am guided from my higher, spiritual self", "I feel connected to the universe" and "I am an extension of the universe" are all great. Last but not least, in yoga you should select meditative postures, such as those of lotus, half lotus and the tree posture.

Now you know how to open your chakras and pursue your sexuality and creativity.

Useful Exercises to Add to Your Morning Ritual

Your body is sacred. It needs to be honored and respected at the deepest level. Don't let anyone tell you otherwise. If you want to elevate your sexuality and enjoy the benefits of seduction, you can do that through specific exercises. In fact, you can add those exercises to your morning ritual and resort to them, whenever you are in need of guidance.

- An interesting thing that you can do to ignite that sexual energy within your body is to get a diary or a blank piece of paper and write down the word "Seductress". This is what you are trying to unlock, after all, your inner seductress, which magnetizes others and makes you feel unstoppable. Then, after that you can start writing down words that you find relevant to the "Seductress". What connotations does that word bring to you? Do that and you will see that the spark will be fuelled. You will get these words and embody them, rather than just have them in your mind. They will be released and you will have the chance to skyrocket your sexuality.

- Sensuality can be boosted through another helpful exercise. You sit down cross legged and you start breathing slowly. Inhale and exhale without haste. Then you can move in a clockwork direction, breathing in as you move inward and breathing out as you move outward. After you have felt that sensual energy working for you, do the reverse. This movement will create sexual energy. As soon as we realize we have created enough energy to serve our purpose, we allow ourselves to feel it. Again, cross legged we slide our upper body to the front and then to the back, without moving our pelvis. Finally, we breathe deeply as we attempt to experience the energy we have created.
- Pelvic floor exercise is another wonderful option that boosts your sexuality and creativity. You lay down on the floor, making sure you have a rug or a mat below you. A pillow can be placed right below your thighs or underneath your knees. Open your hands, get your feet stepping on the ground, knees folded. You must ground your body now. Start with the shoulders, paying attention to your breathing at the same time. Lower the shoulders a tiny bit, and continue on with the spine. Feel it lengthen, sinking in underneath the surface. Then move forward with your hips and thighs, calves and heels. First focus on the right side and then the left one. Following that, feel the light shining all over your body and direct the light beams to your pelvic area. As you inhale, the light sinks deeper and moves closer to your pelvis. Squeeze and release power. Now think of this. The light you have felt within your pelvis becomes a bloomed

rose. What do you do? You sit comfortably, allowing more space for the flower. Slowly, take deep breaths and repeat this expansive movement. When you feel complete, return to your initial position and experience that precious relaxation.

7
EMBRACING YOUR FEMININITY

In this chapter I am going to focus on femininity as a virtue, urging you to embrace it and be proud of who you are. I am guessing by now that you have realized what femininity is all about. You are seeking to find ways to release femininity to the world. Your coming out of the closet as a true feminine might fill you with fear and anxiety. Modern society is not exactly keen on women who have embraced their feminine style. On the contrary, there are often references to women that make them seem like caricatures; many are ridiculed for what they do in their life. Too many stereotypes have developed over the years. A feminine woman dresses in pink, is somewhat silly or superficial, does not have physical power, and relies on the masculine for help.

However, femininity is so much more than that. You should not be afraid to show off your feminine side. Instead, you should embrace it, because it is your superpower. Without it, you would be ordinary and blunt. Thanks to femininity, you are elegant and stylish, you are sensitive and caring, you are smart and full of confidence, hopes and dreams, you are wonderful. Unless you stop relying on what other people think, you can never expect to free your mind and release your true power into the world. Believe it, now that your awakening is taking place, you can really thrive and enjoy your life more.

Your feminine energy determines a lot about yourself. If you enjoy being a woman, then there is no reason to withhold that pleasure. It is your right to shape your personality the way you like. Why would you ever suppress your real feelings? There is no reason to feel guilt or shame due to the long lasting discriminations we have suffered from. Times have changed and this is our moment. No matter how severely you have been traumatized, no matter how much shame you have felt in the past, this is the time to let go and believe in your unique feminine energy. Dare to be feminine, despite what others might say. Who cares, really?

I understand that some women may reject femininity, due to a traumatic situation they have experienced in the past. This is a defensive mechanism and you should not depend on that. Do not waste your life, settling for something that makes you feel less happy than you would be feeling through the release of your feminine energy. Maculine characteristics are typically considered better, in terms of safety and tradition. Most people would prefer them over the more sensitive feminine traits.

In order for you to embrace your femininity, you must first realize where it stems from. To do that, you will need some questions to be answered. So take a moment and think of the answers to the following: "Do you enjoy being a woman?", "What part of femininity do you like and what part makes you feel bad?", "When did you start thinking of femininity?", "Where do you want to be in five years' time?", "Who showed you to be feminine?" and "Are you truly feminine?" are great questions to spark that inner conversation with yourself. It is important to acknowledge your femininity and she when it is lacking. You will find that you are biased against femininity to an extent, due to society's depictions of and discrimination against women.

Now that you have a clearer picture of what femininity actually is, why don't you focus on who has influenced you towards forming your opinion on femininity? If you are afraid of embracing femininity, then probably someone has contributed to your view. It is possible that you have experienced discrimination in the family or at school or by your peers. Things get worse when the people we look up to the most turn out to be judgmental. In this way, we often change our point of view and suppress our own beliefs, so as to keep them pleased and satisfied.

Even in the case of trauma, you can reframe your femininity. This happens through a process you can do on your own. I know that you have been hurt, due to the fact we live in a patriarchal society. Nevertheless, there are aspects of femininity that you are still drawn to. There are details which make you want to be feminine. Find out which qualities are and stick to them. Being a feminine is not just being girly. You are creative and beautiful, you are nurturing and caring.

Women have all of these impressive qualities, making them divine. We are truly unique in the world. Ever since mankind came to exist, women thrived and were worshiped for their qualities. They were worshiped for everything they represented. Their connection to divinity, their healing powers, their compassion and their insight, their empathy and intuition, their wisdom and affection, these were elements that raised women to the pedestal they belonged to. However, things were bound to change. Men were threatened by the dominance of women. They felt lesser and lesser every day, and they could not stand that. This has been the driving force behind the establishment of patriarchy. Through accusations, false interpretations, sabotage, and confrontation, men took over power.

A lot of time has passed since the time period in which patriarchy became the norm in societies across the globe. Women were forced to compromise for less, until they started claiming more. This happened through feminism. This movement rocked the foundations of modern societies and brought huge changes in the way both sexes interact. Nonetheless, there is a major difference we cannot ignore. Through feminism, what women claimed and received was relevant to masculine traits, not feminine ones. Women were eager to live their lives as men, which they have pretty much accomplished so far. But has it been for their own good? I wouldn't think so! Women wanted to imitate masculine behavior, although their purpose is entirely different. We are entirely different. In fact, we complement men, we don't antagonize them and we don't want to be them. Both the feminine and masculine values are beautiful, so we should not abolish either.

You have come to terms with femininity and you are looking forward to implementing it into your daily life. There are millions of ways for you to do that. Pick the ones you really enjoy and go for it. Start paying attention to what you are wearing, so that each outfit represents who you are in a feminine way. Then, you can redecorate your home or just your personal space. You can reorganize the kitchen or change your haircut, dye your hair or start polishing your nails. Tiny details can work wonders towards changing the way you feel inside, as well as the way you look and radiate.

DRIVING MEN WILD

Do you enjoy being a woman? Then your feminine side is celebrated and cherished. This is good. You should know that expressing your feminine energy drives men wild! There are many things that you can do, so as to skyrocket their libido and make them want you like crazy. The best part is that you don't have to pretend. You simply let go of your sensuality and adjust your behavior slightly, in order to appeal to them more than they have ever imagined. Let's have a closer look at some useful tips, which will allow you to get your man thinking of nobody else but you, 24/7.

First and foremost, you need to be comfortable in your femininity. Slow down your breathing, be soft and warm. There is no point in dressing sexy, if you cannot support that without feeling awkward. You are meant to do things you like, not things that others find attractive. Nobody should suppress you and that includes yourself. Instead, make sure that you are comfortable in elegant outfits, pay attention to your hair and makeup, do things that boost your confidence and self esteem. In this way, not only will you look great, but you will also feel like a million dollars.

Next, you should be able to say "no". In the beginning, you might feel bad about turning down a suggestion or sticking to your own plans, rather than adjusting to your partner's routine. However, think of it a little differently. As a woman, you may have thought that you ought to be submissive. This is not the case! You have your own life. You are empowered and independent. So you can have your own interests, your likes and dislikes. If you are too tired to go out tonight, then you should stay home and take a long bath. Don't push yourself to the limits, simply because you want to please your man. He will understand that. In fact, he will be delighted to see that you don't depend on him. The odds are that you will make him want you even more, after having refused a couple of times to go out.

Similar to the above tip, you can make a few compromises, but only after letting him know about them. For instance, you can try out Mexican food, even if you have never thought about doing that due to the spices. "Normally, I would never go to a Mexican restaurant, but I am going to make an exception for you." seems like a great compliment to him. "I usually prefer hiking, but sure, we can go mountain biking if you want. I can try this!", "Hm, I always get a martini, but now I will try what you are having for the first time." are just a few of the ways in which you can make him feel special. Since he is making you experiment with something different for the first time, he is extraordinary, right?

Next thing you can do is to allow your man to do something for you. I know this sounds almost like nothing you have ever been taught in life. Us women have learned the hard way to be strong and independent, expressing our masculine energy whenever possible. Nevertheless, you need to twist that a little, just as a reminder that you are feminine and you are in need of protection. There is nothing wrong in appearing vulnerable at times. Of course, you should not go to extremes and come across as helpless. Just a tiny bit. "Oh how thoughtful of you to cook dinner, I am too tired to cook for myself and

I am famished!", "Thank you for buying the groceries because I forgot about it" are wonderful ways to let him know he is needed.

The key component to making your man want you beyond comparison is to give him space and time. You know, we tend to react differently to men and this has its roots to science. Men don't process cortisol hormone like women, which makes them more prone to bursting with emotions. This is why men are more likely to snap and lose control. When you think of the way your man responds to you, it is really important that you take this into account. Otherwise, you will feel like he is not treating you right. So if you are willing to let that steam off and allow your man some breathing space, he will appreciate it a great deal. He will see that you are getting him, which will make him get closer to you eventually.

You should never rely on a man for your happiness. This is totally independent, since you can be happy on your own. Attracting a man should be all about fun, and it should be a part of your divine self expression. Always keep that in mind and be generous with your divine feminine energy, letting your man see what lies beneath the surface and introducing him to the wonders lying ahead. He will be crazy about you in no time!

Sexual Energy Activation and Nurturing

Your sexual energy should be celebrated, because you are entitled to absolute passion and pleasure. Why would you want to suppress your needs? Your sensuality will guide you to the highest levels of awareness, offering you the opportunity to enjoy life like you have never before. So you must find ways to activate and nurture your sexual energy, so that it grows and expands from within. There are many things you can do, as long as you realize that the energy should be contained within you to give its maximum potential.

First off, we start with food. Yes, whatever we eat affects us in more ways than we can imagine. This means that you need to pay attention to what you eat, not only to maintain your ideal weight and remain healthy. Each food you choose will influence the quality of your sexual energy. Feel free to eat fresh vegetables and fruit as much as possible, ensuring that you get most of that food raw. Avoid processed foods, artificial sweeteners and colorings, heavy cream, and too much fat.

Instead, appreciate flavor and texture. Choose quality over quantity and make every bite count. As for liquids, drink a lot of water and indulge in green and herbal tea, as well as moscato wine several times a day. This will bring you closer to divinity, so see if you enjoy the taste. I am sure you will!

Then, pamper yourself as much as you can. Have a long bath with salts and essential oils, clearing your mind from anything unnecessary. Get rid of the tension with a nice massage, meditate or engage in yoga sessions. Go out for a walk, take in the fresh air, and feel the calmness surrounding you. Take some time off, dedicate it to yourself and make the most of every moment. We have been used to squeezing in as many things as we can within the day. However, this only fills us with anxiety and we are always left feeling incomplete. At the end of the day, what matters is that we have pleased ourselves, we have done our best, and we have connected to the ones we love.

Have you ever tried mystical dance? This is the best way to dance from within you, so that you awaken the divine feminine energy. You need to understand the chakras of your body and release the tension, expanding the energy. Belly dance is an excellent form of mystical dance, so you can try it out and see what it brings out to you. The three steps to truly embrace your sexual energy and express it to the world include ways to relax, ignite the energy, and then contain it. So after having relaxed through deep breathing techniques, meditation and positive affirmations, you can ignite the energy through belly dance. Starting from the backbone and the first chakra, you can communicate with the universe through your body. Feel the energy expanding and moving upward, but keep it contained. This will help you experience energy at its fullest potential, without dispersing it into the world. Keep it within you, treasure it and enjoy.

Once you have done that, you will feel empowered and ready to take on the world. No more boundaries holding you back from enjoyment, no more taboos to overcome. You deserve to experience the full magnitude of pleasure deriving from your sexual energy, in alignment with the universe.

Antagonizing Men: Is This Real?

As I pointed out earlier in the book, there is absolutely no reason why you should antagonize men and compare yourself to them. In fact, if there is one thing we have learned so far about human relationships, it is the acknowledgement that both men and women should create the perfect balance to thrive together. Just like Yin and Yang, you need to find the right proportions to accomplish the ideal unity. Yin energy can be found in the calmness of subtle colors and soft music, and in the relaxation derived from the water gently flowing into the sea. On the other hand, there is Yang energy, which is far more active and can be seen in more intense light, colors and sounds. There is no comparison between the two energies, only an effort to balance and create something beautiful in the world.

Women have been misled to believe that they need to antagonize men, trying to outrank them, and reclaim what they have lost. This is a vicious cycle, since it strips women of their uniqueness and shows no actual desire to find harmony in life. A woman should not look at men and try to be more like them. Obviously, as discussed before, there are masculine aspects and characteristics in each individual, including women. However, this does not mean that a woman ought to change her very essence and let those masculine traits prevail. In this way, she will lose the divine feminine energy, which is vital for her well being and the celebration of her identity.

When a man and a woman are joined together, a true miracle takes place. There are forces so different, yet complementing one another. You don't need to do your best, in pursuit of proving that you are better than men. This is not a race, nor a competition. Nevertheless, you should stand your ground and claim what you want. You have the power to lay the foundations for a fruitful relationship, which is based on mutual understanding, love, and affection. Do not try to spoil that, by proving your point or sticking to feelings of revenge and spite. This is not who you are. Your union should be a blessing, rather than a constant conflict. Remember the Law of Polarity (Create Balance And Harmony Using the Law of Polarity, 2016). According to this acknowledgement, for every action there is an equal reaction of the same size and intensity. Everything in life comes with two poles, for example, good and evil. Everything is in fact dual in life. This means that we people are in search of our second pole to feel whole again. What we manifest is a combination of the two poles, trying to acquire balance. You should not forget that.

Men are not the enemy here. If anything, they should be our allies. We are in this together. They are as lost as we are, in the journey towards enlightenment and personal awareness. We dive deep inside and we try to explore the unknown. Both men and women seek harmony in a relationship. It is only fair to assume that this harmony can be reached through profound understanding, as well as the realization that we are not the same. We are equal, but not the same. Nobody is superior; instead, our value is identical. This is how we are meant to structure a solid relationship, which is going to make the relationship last, despite the toll of time.

8

RELEASE PAST TRAUMA AND MAKE SPACE FOR YOUR DIVINE FEMININE AWAKENING

Ever since you were a little girl, you were told to change the way that you behaved. At the same time, any sign of femininity that you showed seems to have triggered negative reactions. Does that sound familiar? When you are not certain of yourself and your identity, you grow up questioning everything. You question your power and your personal value, you doubt whether you are worthy enough to trigger love and pleasure, you shy away from anything that makes you feel and look womanly. But is this really the way to be? Do you truly want to compromise everything, just to fit in the generic boxes others have created for you?

It feels wrong to live your life according to what others dictate. Especially when your life is so unique and you are able to experience greatness and divinity. First, you need to clear out trauma from your past, shifting your mindset and resetting your life. You must delve into deep research and unlearn what you have been taught all these years. It requires a lot of effort and hard work, but I promise it is worth it. What you need to do is to unearth and ground yourself in your truth. It is what you believe and what you want that matters the most.

You have been wounded deeply, your feminine side has been traumatized and now you are experiencing the side effects of this trauma. Maybe your sexual identity has become a matter of criticism, a reason to feel ashamed. Everyone around you has been looking at you like you are nothing but a vessel of sexual pleasure. Your figure triggers desires and this is perfectly OK for men. They can express that desire, without paying attention to your emotions. Whether you feel comfortable or not, they can comment on the way you look, and they can make their move, even if it causes you distress.

On the other hand, you are always advised to be solemn and subtle. You should not be aggressive or provoke men, because then you will have it coming. In society, a woman who is liberated and expresses her femininity is almost always considered provocative. She should slow down, cover her true self, and settle for society's standards as to what is acceptable and what isn't. This can lead to a hyper sense of sexuality. So instead of feeling comfortable and fine being sexy, you use that to manipulate others. You know that this is a tool, an advantage you have over men. Why not use it to your benefit? More than that, you seduce and control men with the most powerful thing on you—because this is what you have been taught to believe.

The other way in which trauma can appear in your life is through suppressed emotions. To be more specific, you have always heard others telling you to be tough. Us women are often characterized as too soft, powerless, and unable to control our emotions. It is absolutely understandable why women are more sensitive. It is in their feminine side of existence. However, society does not have room for that. On the contrary, women are expected to toughen up and endure hardships, as well as negative feelings, without complaining. It is a cruel world, but you need to pull through and find ways to cope with that. Moreover, we are told that we should be more like men. What does a man do when something bad comes along? He deals with it, no crying, no whining.

With that in mind, you learn how to suppress your emotions while you are growing up. You undervalue their meaning and you become accustomed to imitating masculine behavior. There is nothing wrong in having a masculine side. In fact, having the perfect balance between masculine and feminine would be the right way to live your life. But this doesn't mean that you should forget what it's like to be a woman. Showing compassion, being sensitive and open, warm and soft—these are all elements that define who you really are. These traits reveal your greatness and they should not be forgone.

UNBURDEN YOURSELF FROM HEAVY BAGGAGE

Unrooting past traumas to make space for your divine feminine awakening is of the essence. You need to be strong and take all the necessary steps so that you can move forward. When you have so much weight on your shoulders, it is only fair that you feel overwhelmed and exhausted. On the contrary, once you deal with the issues that have been troubling you and get your closure, you will feel lighter than ever before. So do not waste any more time. Find what is dragging you down and get rid of it at once. You ought to deal with these issues by clearing the subconscious beliefs that you have as a woman, and this book will not only help you become aware of your limiting beliefs, but also move through them. Healing the inner child can make space for your awakening.

The first thing you need to do is to confront the trauma. It is imperative that you address clearly what has traumatized you, because otherwise you cannot deal with it properly. When you are facing an unknown threat, there is no effective way to overcome the problem and move past it. So confrontation is the key to success. If you keep burying it underground, then you will only prolong a negative situation and prevent yourself from experiencing what you are entitled to. Do not hide yourself from the truth; do not conceal the facts or distort reality.

Next, you should talk about what happened. There is great flexibility in how to achieve that. Some people might choose therapy, because they feel like trusting a professional. Of course, this is a good thing. The experts will guide you through the process of analyzing the details regarding your trauma. Through proper questions, you will have the opportunity to read in between the lines and see exactly what has triggered your wound. Was it a specific incident or was it a person that made you feel bad? Alternatively, women can turn to their friends for releasing their tension and letting off some steam. Family can serve exactly the same way, although most people think family members may pressure trauma victims into not opening up. Last but not least, a journal can be quite liberating. So if you express yourself in writing, you can try out gathering your thoughts in a diary.

Moving forward, it is time to accept what has happened. This is the only way for you to find your peace. Although it can make you feel pain, you need to go through that pain to recover. You should be ready to accept that everything happens for a reason. Holding on to the past will destroy your life. It will be an anchor, which drives you to the bottom. You need to get rid of the anchor's chain, so as to emerge back on the surface. Use that trauma as a lesson and not as a pattern. Finally, you have completed the cycle and you are ready to move on. No more excuses, no more alibi for suffering. You are free.

Easy to Follow Morning Ritual

What do you do when you wake up in the morning? Are you one of these people, who sets a dozen alarms, only to click on the "snooze" button? This is only buying you a fraction of the time you should be sleeping, you know that, right? Or maybe you stand up right after the first alarm has rung, so as to get ready and head to work? Whatever you do, chances are that you do not devote much time to yourself. Too bad! Your soul needs nourishment, as much as your body does. Therefore, you need to take care of your mental clarity and your calmness. To do that, you will need to change some old vices of yours.

By shifting your habits, you will discover a whole new world. In this way, you will be able to experiment with new patterns that might become your favorite. First off, you must commit to waking up slightly earlier than what you would have hoped. This will allow you to wake up more naturally, avoiding tension and unnecessary stress. Then, you should prepare yourself a hearty and healthy breakfast. It is essential that you get hydrated, letting your body replenish all the valuable components it lost overnight. Find out which foods really agree with your digestive system, while at the same time offering you the nutrients and energy you need for a full day ahead.

Next, you must incorporate some sort of physical exercise in your morning ritual. Obviously, it is best that you practice meditation and special exercises, meant to trigger different parts of your body. However, you must also find the time to appreciate the moment and let go of the stress. This is the perfect way to start your day. Back to exercise, you should implement a daily feminine morning ritual that focuses on clearing trauma, limiting self beliefs, shame and realigning with your sacred feminine energy. There are quite a few different techniques and sets of exercises that you can try out. Below, you will find some really helpful and easy exercises which you can fit in your daily schedule. Start your day with this workout and you will feel refreshed, regenerated and filled with energy.

First off, we start with TRE exercises. TRE stands for Trauma Releasing Exercises. If you observe the animal kingdom, you will notice a lot of animals do that to shake off any tension. The same applies to humans, so you should really experiment with the power of shaking off the trauma from your body. One of the best exercises to do is to stand up and move your back towards the wall. Then you should slowly move your body downward, while making your legs create an angle and opening them slightly. So in the end, it will be like you are sitting on an invisible chair, supporting your body through the back and mainly through the legs. As soon as you feel that you are on the brink of collapsing due to the weight, you get a little higher and you continue working out like that. After having almost resumed your initial standing position, you will feel your muscles tremor. You must then lie down on your back, knees raised, with the bottom your feet planted firmly on the floor a few inches apart. Experiment with moving your knees apart to discover what creates the most intense shaking. This will release stored trauma in your body. I practice TRE at least 30 minutes a day and have felt huge results! To stay productive, I often read while shaking out.

If you want a different TRE exercise, then you can lay down and connect your feet, while bending your legs. Now your position will be like that of a frog. When you feel comfortable with that, try to raise your body towards the sky. This is an excellent exercise for toning up your muscles as well. While you are staying in that position, you will realize that the muscles are burning. Tighten up your buttocks, and feel the muscles getting strained. Repeat as many times as it takes, so as to promote the tremor. You will be impressed by the results. Once again, you must allow time to shake out in the lying position.

EFT exercises stand for Emotional Freedom Techniques. When you are feeling overwhelmed by stress or anxiety, depression or even chronic pain, this can work wonders for you. The whole concept is based on alternative medicine like acupuncture, neuro-linguistic programming, and a lot more. It would be great to add some EFT exercises in your morning ritual. This involves tapping specific parts of your body, while keeping a steady rhythm and repeating positive affirmations. In this case, you can start tapping the external part of your palm and then move on your face. The spot underneath your eyes, on your cheeks, right below your nose, on your chin, on your ribs and just below your armpits—these are all exceptional spots to practice EFT tapping. Type EFT tapping into YouTube and there are hundreds of results! I personally focus on one tapping video until I feel that issue resolve on my life. For example, if I am feeling shame during a particular week, I will focus primarily on a shame EFT tapping video that week, or until I have cleared it.

As for what you can say, try something similar to the following: "I have been through a lot of pressure. There is trauma in my life, which has messed with my entire being. I have been hurt, I have cried, and I have suffered enough. Now it is my time to shine. I am powerful enough to leave this trauma behind. It is within my power to fight back and overcome the hardship that has happened to me. I am strong and wonderful." This is just an example, so that you can experiment with what makes you feel better. Add positive affirmations, which will help you build on your confidence and see who you really are. You better believe it!

9
GRASP YOUR DIVINE FEMININE AWAKENING

Nobody was born knowing all the answers to their questions. And there is one particular question which has been on your mind for quite some time now. Of course, this has been one of the main reasons why you have got your hands on this book. You are searching for the answers, which will enlighten you as to your journey towards divine feminine awakening. We are all humans and humans need answers. We are in need of positive feedback and confirmation that we are on the right path. However, there is not a clear "yes or no" verdict. You cannot visit a professional to get diagnosed as awakening or not, can you? So in moments of doubt, you must turn to whoever holds the wisdom and knowledge to guide you.

Are you wondering whether or not your divine feminine is finally awakening? There are times when we feel over the moon, only to find out that we have been deceived by the signs. Especially when it comes to discovering your divine power, the stakes are way too high. I understand that you are feeling anticipation to experience what is about to come. But is that truly happening? Are you indeed on your way to experience this wonderful feeling? Are you about to turn over a new leaf? I am going to offer you a plethora of signs, so that you know your imagination is not playing tricks on you. If you tick more than a few of these boxes, then you are indeed waking up. So are you ready to identify hese tell tale signs?

Obviously, one of the fundamental signs that you are waking up is your deepest intuition. You will feel it in your bones. You will be sure that something is changing, just like a caterpillar which is about to turn into a butterfly. This transformation is huge and will happen from within. Have you ever felt certain about anything in your life? For those of you who have felt so in love that anything else doesn't matter, this will be quite similar. Have you ever met women who have decided to change their life against all odds, because they felt right? Or maybe you are one of these women? This is the feeling, so look out for that sign as an amuse bouche, the perfect start to a delectable meal ahead!

ARE YOU WAKING UP FROM YOUR HIBERNATION?

Your feminine divine power is slowly waking up, so how can you tell? One of the things that should alarm you is the fact that you are always digging deeper, in pursuit of the real "you". It is a great thing to try and figure out who you are, meaning that you don't know. This self doubt reveals that you are much more than what you thought you were. The more you discover about yourself, the more you get to love your uniqueness. You cherish it and embrace it. There is nothing better than knowing you don't fit any boxes, but you are extraordinary and special.

At the same time, you get rid of selfishness. There is no "ego" in the picture. As a Starseed, you have been incarnated in this life to lay the world a helping hand. You are meant to offer, rather than act on egoism and personal interests. This doesn't mean that you forget to love yourself—not at all. One of the signs that you are on your way to your awakening is the fact that you take great care of yourself. Who is more precious than you, after all? As a matter of fact, you will be prone to improving your diet and making some radical changes about your wellness. For instance, you will want to quit smoking or give up on sugar, coffee or fat altogether.

Moving on with the signs that should alert you you are on the route to success, you will notice a significant shift in the way you treat others. Until now you have been accustomed to bending the knee, whenever there was a conflict. You pretty much did what others expected of you. It feels like you didn't have your own will. But now, you feel it in your gut that something has changed. Now you don't worry about what others might say. The protagonist in your own movie is you and you alone. What is more, you no longer succumb to patriarchal concepts. Even if you have learned all your life to follow these rules, they no longer speak to you. You know better than that.

As we discussed earlier in the book, you leave all those bitter experiences in the past. You don't hold grudges, nor do you fall back into the same traps. This is the past; what is done is done. Now a potential setback cannot be used as an excuse to shape the future in a negative pattern. So you let go of all the worrisome experiences, all the mistakes and all the misconceptions. Of course, this doesn't mean that you should beat yourself up. Contrary to what you may think, one of the signs has to do with compassion towards yourself and forgiveness. You have done nothing wrong, after all. Life does not come with its own manual, so trial and error is totally allowed.

Well, you should be prepared for all these good things coming your way, letting you in on the secret you are finally waking up. Nevertheless, it is not all roses and sunshine. This is an enormous shift in your life, which will definitely make you feel scared. You will be frightened at the thought that nothing should be taken for granted. On the contrary, you must always be ready to doubt even the very core of your existence. Is everything you have lived so far a lie? This can bring you down, causing depression and even suicidal thoughts. Please be patient, you will get through this. It is meant to be an extraordinary experience, which only a few are ever going to enjoy in life. Don't feel helpless, as you are nothing like that.

It makes sense that you will feel the need to share your experience with others. Being awakened and knowing it takes a lot of courage. In order to deal with the changes that happen all the time, you should find your community. Hence, you will feel the urge to find your peers. You will want to explore the places, where you can meet like minded people to talk about everything you have been experiencing. There is nothing alarming about that. In fact, we all require support at times. On the bright side, despite what you may initially think, you will eventually restore your hope. Besides, you have been blessed and this is something to celebrate, rather than frown upon.

Over time, the signs you see become clearer and clearer. Your confidence strengthens, as you are beginning to realize what is truly taking place. It is not rare for people like you to have breakthroughs and epiphanies. Things will start making sense, as you are connecting all the dots. You will soon feel more powerful than ever, certain about where you are heading. Although self-hatred could have crept in, filling you with disappointment, you loathe yourself no more. How could you? You are sacred, believe in that. Your ego is transformed, your chakras are unblocked, and you feel ready for your new life.

Way to Go, Girl!

If you have made it that far, you most likely have experienced those early awakening signs in your life, so congratulations! This is an amazing journey, which has just begun. Take a moment and sink it in, trying to fully perceive what is going on. You are the chosen, you are sacred, you are unique. No one is going to take that power away from you, because you won't let them. You are in control of your emotions, you are in control of your entity. Imagine the full potential of releasing your divine feminine energy into the world. Let it flow right through you and feel what it can do. You are divine and no one can take that away from you. Your power has been there all along, but you have not been able to see that. Now you know and it is only fair that you change your life, based on your recent revelations.

Your instinct was right. That voice in your head, which kept telling you not to give up, is now shouting out with joy and excitement. This is your moment, girl. You ought to be proud of yourself. You have come this far, interpreting the signs and pursuing your dreams and hopes. Some people would say you were overly enthusiastic, some others would call you crazy. Doubting others and making them feel bad is something most people resort to when they feel threatened. And being different always poses a threat to others. But this doesn't mean you should look forward to uniformity. You did not give in to the temptation to please others by changing your personality. What you did took courage, and you lived up to the expectations.

It has been a rocky road, for sure. I imagine that most people were not there by your side. During your explorations, many of your so-called friends and family did nothing but judge you. They have been questioning your motives and they have been looking down on you ever since you have expressed your need to delve into this soul-searching experience. Many people find it hard to get rid of their old beliefs. They stick to what they know and they are inflexible, leaving no room for the tiniest bit of change. These are the first to doubt you, even when you have evidence to back up your claims.

Through the hardships, you managed to rise from the ashes like the phoenix. You have persisted in your goals and found what you were looking for. All these people who did not hesitate to call you names and shame you, make fun of you or even isolate you socially—where are they now? Are they close to you, so as to witness your transformation? I certainly hope they get to see what has become of you. It is going to be a memorable day, when you feel indifferent toward their attitudes and actions. Just remember, your divinity is unquestionable. You are sacred and nobody should tell you otherwise.

Your efforts have undoubtedly persevered through hardship. All these results have come through sweat and tears. This only makes your victory sweeter. You know that you have persisted in your goals, even when everyone around you told you to quit. Not only did you not listen to their advice, but you pushed yourself to experience your awakening and enjoy what lies ahead. It is a wonder that you survived, a wonder that you have orchestrated on your own. You deserve congratulations, as a way to express my gratitude for not giving up. Us women must empower one another and help each other to overcome any shadows or low points during this demanding process. Congratulations for what you have achieved thus far, we are all looking forward to what comes up next.

There is greatness ahead for you, dear. The road will not be paved with roses, but you have been forged with fire and steel. You can take on any challenge that comes your way. Now, one final sign to look for. I am sure it is already there. Your third eye is open, isn't it? Focus and see right through, see what it unveils for you. Exciting times, truly exciting times ahead...

10

GUIDED MEDITATIONS TO TAKE YOU BY THE HAND

There are several guided meditations that you can do to experience your divine awakening, and they will make the difference in your life. Among them, feel free to find the meditations that actually speak to you. The feminine energy awakening guided meditation is the first meditation which we are going to focus on in this section. It allows you to empower yourself and become the woman you have always dreamed of being.

You start by sitting comfortably on the floor, using a blanket or a soft mat. You stretch a little, making sure that all your muscles are relaxed. You place your palms in your lap. Focus on your breath, noticing how the air flows inside and then outside. Now it is time to focus on connecting with your inner feminine energy. Begin to become aware of a pink rose, which is blooming inside your heart. Pay attention to each petal, watching as the rose begins to grow and expand. The rose is getting bigger and wider with your every breath. Now your awareness should be on the top of your head, and you may be experiencing a slight tingling sensation.

As you are watching this, soft pink light illuminates you. It bathes you from the top of your head all the way down to your hips and legs. This is all you see, pink light that symbolizes pure love. This is awakening your feminine energy. You bring light into your darkness, as the Goddess within you guides you without judgment. Slowly, you are starting to come to terms with unconditional acceptance. Notice her powerful presence washing over you. The powerful feminine energy is awakening, feeling the change in your physical body, your mind and your heart. This is a transformation that you welcome.

Picture yourself on top of the mountain, with the air blowing softly, and touching your cheeks, fondling your hair. Stay fully connected to your inner goddess, bringing this awareness back to where you are now. Open your eyes slowly, feeling the tips of your fingers and toes, lowering your shoulders. This is how you get closer to your feminine energy, awakening it to enjoy the maximum benefits that can be derived from this unpretentious flow.

BALANCING MASCULINE AND FEMININE ENERGIES GUIDED MEDITATION

Through the balancing masculine and feminine energies guided meditation, you will be able to reach out to your oneness and experience completion, absolute balance and a sense of pure wellbeing. This is a marvelous way to get closer to both your sides, stop fighting one another and enjoy the best of the masculine, and the feminine, sides within you.

You sit comfortably somewhere and start to breathe in and out, really gently and slowly. Let go of your worries and everything that has been troubling you. Close your eyes and go to a peaceful place, travel somewhere you feel comfortable and set out on your new journey. This can be a familiar place, or a place you have never seen before in your life. Let the colors embrace you, soothing your soul. What colors surround you? See yourself, as you are glowing with an immense light. You are radiant. Notice all the details about yourself. Are you small or big, are you beautiful, radiant, elegant? Take a moment and concentrate on your chakras. Which of those chakras are already glowing in your body? All your different energy centers should start glowing, so pay attention to those that are not quite there yet.

Now, look in the distance. There is another being coming towards you, a being of the opposite sex in a radiant form. As the being gets closer and closer, you realize that you are equally beautiful, equally radiant, equally sized. You are the exact opposite polarity, but everything else is similar. Greet that being with your palms, approaching even more. Your palms touch and then slowly you begin merging. As you are becoming one, you feel that energy igniting you. There is an awakening of the opposite traits, the opposite energy within you. Your masculine energy is spiked and complements your feminine traits. Doesn't it feel wonderful?

The presence of this other being ignites the central column of your body, which offers you the chance to experience the absolute balance between your masculine and feminine energies. The union of these two distinct energies connects you to that higher power. Finally, it is time for that being to flow out of your body and leave. This allows you to remain who you are. However, you have the opportunity to merge whenever you feel like doing so. You can come to this place in your mind anytime and experience the same thing. To regain consciousness and wake up, start breathing deeply, and move your toes and fingers slightly.

Reiki Goddess Guided Meditation

If you are having trouble sleeping, or if you are overly stressed, and you want to release the tension, the Reiki Goddess guided meditation is a superb option for you.

Close your eyes and breathe deeply. Let go, as you set out on a journey to the most powerful landscapes. In fact, you are floating and you can feel your feet slowly ascending to the skies. There, you find the Goddess. As you are exhaling, you free your mind and think of a tale about time. Time started giving orders to the planets, the solar system, the different galaxies, as Hope breathed life into them. The Temptress instilled her blessings and curiosity started sinking in, so Time moved faster and faster. More and more stars were added to the night sky, offering their immense glow to the universe. Then, Time moved even faster and colors spread all over the world. Thousands of chromatic shades, lovely hues in perfect harmony, creating masterpieces of nature.

Time could not stand still, so every heartbeat sounded like music and motivated time to move faster and faster. As Time wandered through the universe, it stumbled upon a Sun. The Sun had no beat, unlike everything else in the world. So it had no knowledge of its birth, no curiosity to find out, no blessing whatsoever. With the Sun shining brightly and giving its warmth to the universe, Time had to slow down. Time could not even move, so he literally contained himself while trying to move round the Sun. Now Time was yearning for love, but love was nowhere to be found. He could not join the rest of the universe, listen to the beat, and feel the curiosity necessary for him to continue on hus trajectory.

In response to Time's yearning, the universe created the Goddess of Love. She came to Time's rescue and sat on his left shoulder. So, having Time by her side, the Goddess of Love began teaching the Sun. She sang sweetly, while butterflies filled her hands, and bee honey aromas filled the atmosphere. Her voice and singing was healing. The Goddess then took the Sun and neatly placed everything in the universe just so to bring all into balance. The planets, the moons, the shooting stars, the suns, and everything was in perfect sync to produce the most magnificent outcome.

The Goddess of Love talked to the Sun, explaining that there is a special beat within each and every single one of us. If you truly listen, you will be able to hear that special tune, the beat that keeps us in harmony with the rest of the universe. This beat comes in the form of the heart.

FEMININE INNER CHILD HEALING GUIDED MEDITATION

Your family raised you in a certain way, often going above and beyond to do what is right. They protected and cherished you, they nourished and provided for you. However, this doesn't mean that you are left unwounded by the process of growing up. There are traumas that lie there beneath the surface and hold you back from enjoying life to the fullest. When you indulge in the inner child healing meditation, it will help you to ease and resolve past traumas. Let us see how you can practice this meditation.

You begin by closing your eyes. You take a deep, calm breath. Slow down, unwind and relax. Lower your shoulders a bit, let them fall a little bit. Your entire body falls lower. Then you start thinking of your past, your life as a child. You visualize it and think of all the negativity, all the bad situations that have brought you to where you are now, traumatized and helpless. You should have found protection and reassurance, but you didn't. Next, visualize your life's timeline. There is a light at the end of the timeline, and you are getting closer to it. With every breath you take, feel the light surrounding you, warming you, illuminating every cell of your body.

Imagine that the vortexes on the bottom of your feet open so that they receive the same light from mother earth. Now you feel lighter and healthier than ever, it is time to look back to the dysfunctional behavior that led to your trauma. Try to identify where it began. Keep your eyes closed, feeling the warm energy overwhelming you. You are ready to travel back to your childhood. Once you locate that very moment, open the door right in front of you. What you find there is amazing. There is your figure, as well as the figure of yourself as a child.

Observe each other and, when you feel comfortable enough, start talking to your younger self. It is going to be emotional, for sure. Try to reassure the child that everything will be alright. You are the living and breathing manifestation that everything will work out in the end. Take the child in your arms, comfort her, and let her know that you are sorry you couldn't be there for her. Allow dialog between the two. This child is sweet and innocent. Take a few moments, comfort her, and make her feel secure. Notice how innocent and hopeful she is, all she needs is love. Unfortunately, parents or caregivers could not provide that and so the child was programmed in the wrong way.

Then, go ahead and talk to the child. "Sweet little child, I love you. I support you. You are wonderful and you can do anything you set your mind on. I will keep you safe and protected from all harm" Say all the things that you have been longing to hear and no one has ever told you. This will correct the programming for this child. Let them know the negative consequences of their unhealthy patterns. "Sweet child, don't take care of your parents. It is not meant to be this way. Do not listen to what others say. You are kind and worthy, you deserve to be loved. You deserve to be happy. Others projected their fears, their wounds and their problems onto you, and they weren't yours to take. Instead, take care of yourself and yourself, alone."

In the end, you should invite your younger version to come with you, so that you can keep them safe like you promised. Allow the child to climb up and come with you, merging within your current figure. Then, take a few calming, deep breaths, and feel the purifying light within you. Now you can bring forward your past self to your current state, you can erase all the traumas and correct the dysfunctions that have occurred from your childhood. Relax, sigh with relief, and appreciate the moment. You are ready to come back. Feel your toes wiggle and open your eyes. Stretch a little and smile. You have made it to the finish line.

MANIFESTING YOUR BEAUTIFUL LIFE WITH YOUR DIVINE FEMININE ENERGY

Experiencing your divine feminine energy, don't you feel that something has changed in your life? I am not referring to the theoretical changes, but to what happens in your everyday life. After having reached that point where you don't doubt your divinity anymore, a whole new world of potential unfolds. This is where you truly grasp what has happened. Your life will never be the same. What you have been dreaming of all this time, what you have been secretly wishing to happen, is here. What does this mean for you, practically speaking?

There are many things in life that cause anxiety and stress, keeping you from truly appreciating the moment and enjoying your life 100%. Most people stress over money, health and relationships, as well as professional issues. It is in your hands to pick out what is troubling you more in your life, so as to change it according to your desires. You are holding the power required to attract what you are lacking. If you are wondering how you can achieve that, it is quite simple and straightforward. You will need the power of your mind to succeed in flipping your life upside down. Have you ever spent time alone, envisioning how you would have wanted your life to be? There are times when people feel down and they are trying to hold on to something; a memory, a person, a dream. So they often end up fantasizing about their dream life. They imagine how the perfect house would be, along with the perfect partner and the perfect career. Of course, all that comes with a generous amount of money in their bank account. This is by far the best company!

By reaching deep into your divine feminine energy and using it to your benefit, you can create the basis on which to live your dream life. Even if this sounds too good to be true, indeed you can shape your future with the power of your inner goddess. Think carefully and imagine what would make you happy. Then, ask the universe to provide that for you—just wait and see. Before you know it, your entire life will have changed its course. You will be en route to success, any way you define the term. If you ask from your inner goddess to bring you wealth, then you should expect riches to come your way, even without you knowing it. If, however, you have asked for health and wellness, you will feel empowered to improve your diet and workout. You will feel more motivated than ever to stick to your plan, so that you become the healthiest, fittest, happiest version of yourself.

There is nothing stopping you, now that you know the secret. Your divine feminine energy is powerful enough to cause chaos. Of course, this is not what you want. On the contrary, what you are seeking is all about finding harmony and the perfect balance in life. Whatever makes you happy should be given to you in a heartbeat. There is no need to wait and rely on luck. Let us face the truth, luck always favors the bold and daring in life. You should do your part, rather than expect others to come to your rescue. With your inner goddess, there is nobody else you need.

LAW OF ATTRACTION AND FEMININE ENERGY

"When you want something, all the universe conspires in helping you to achieve it" (Paulo Coelho - Wikiquote, n.d.) This is a famous quote from Paulo Coelho, which pretty much sums up what Law of Attraction is. Let us have a look at how the Law of Attraction (The Law Of Attraction - Discover How to Improve Your Life, n.d.), this New Thought Philosophy, can work wonders on our life. Through the use of feminine energy, we can attract what we want and make the most of our desires. In this way, we can pursue wealth, abundance, love, career, and everything else our heart desires, if we use our divine energy properly.

First of all, take a moment and think about it. Have you ever been in a situation when wanting something actually causes you physical pain? Your heart just hurts, because you want something so much. If you have ever watched YouTube videos of children reacting to puppies and kittens, you will know what I mean. As soon as a parent offers the child a puppy, the child bursts out in tears. The emotions are overflowing, making the child unable to restrain themselves. The same happens when you cry joyous tears at the thought of a loved one or in anticipation of an important event. In a similar pattern, your overdesiring leads to self doubt and second guessing as to whether or not this is the right choice for you. Even though you might have spent a lot of time thinking of something, the moment you obtain it, you instantly start doubting that it was the best decision. Both these options mean that you want something more than you are able to allow it. Can you grasp that concept? When you want something in excess, then you end up working against yourself. This will come back like a boomerang and hit you in the face, if you don't pay attention to the signs.

The secret lies in harmony and balance. Without the right balance, you cannot find your inner peace. More than that, you cannot enjoy what you are meant to enjoy in life. Balance that out and then you will be able to pursue what you are craving. Don't get carried away by emotions; instead, set realistic goals and anticipations. Besides, Rome was not built in a day. What does that mean for you? Well, you will need to make peace with where you are right now in order to get to where you want to be. It takes time to reassess your current situation and see how you can improve your life, one step at a time. So it is imperative that you find the silver lining and identify the good things in your current state.

Moving forward, you should not neglect the whole ritual of visualizing what it would feel like to get what you want when it comes to love. As a result, you picture yourself as the receiver and you analyze all the emotions that are sparked by your accomplishments. If you do that frequently, you will get the chance to reap the benefits of your imagination. As you think about your feelings, something truly marvelous happens. You will radiate these feelings to attract the thing you want. It makes sense that your aura attracts those you want and repels those you loathe. If you stick to that plan, you will notice that the wrong people will fade away and the right people will come closer to you. I know that you may be skeptical, but give it a try.

Focus on the things that you think you are lacking. For example, if you are in a bad financial state, then visualize that you are wealthy. Think of your riches, lay down your money, and see how much you have got. Use positive affirmations to convince your mind that you are already wealthy. You own a yacht, you have jewelry and stocks in your safe deposit box, and your bank account has more money than you could ever need in your life. If, on the other hand, you are mostly yearning for love and you are alone, then try to repeat time and over again that you are worthy of love and that your dream partner is right there searching for you. Believe in your ability to attract love and enjoy a wonderful relationship with the man of your dreams. He will come knocking on your door before you know it!

Equally important is for you to address the signs that reveal that you are on the right track towards success. When you lose hope, it makes sense that you find something to lift you up and restore your faith in yourself. What a better way to achieve that than to collect all the evidence that proves that your actions have had a positive impact on you and the rest of the world. It is uplifting to have the proof required, so that you know you are doing great. If you are walking blindfolded, you will always doubt as to whether or not you are moving in the right direction. Once you open your eyes, you instantly get the reassurance that you have been wishing to receive.

When you are actively pursuing a man to indulge in a new relationship, the Law of Attraction can help you out a great deal. Obviously, you first need to make sure that the man you are interested in is actually on the same page as you. I am not talking about being in love with you, but it is only fair to pursue a man who is not married, heterosexual, and open to new acquaintances. Otherwise, your odds will naturally diminish and the law of attraction is not the one to blame here. Then, you should focus on the essence of the man. This means that you should identify what feelings he brings out in you. These feelings are what is driving you to want to be with him. If you are asking yourself why this is a crucial part of forming the relationship, review how the Law of Attraction works. You need to elicit these feelings to yourself first and then from a man.

As an exercise to practice the Law of Attraction and the impact it has on your feminine energy, every morning you can write down whatever you want to happen within your day. This can be as small as enjoying a hearty, delectable meal, or as big as winning the lottery. Some of the things that you include on the list may sound nearly impossible. The same goes for the man of your dreams. Write down if you want to meet him, where you want to see him and what you want him to do. Write everything in detail and put them in a list, so that the universe can provide. Even if at first this all comes across as wishful thinking, you will soon perceive its meaning and true value.

Rather than sitting idle and doing nothing, or wondering why your life has become so stale and bitter, you need to step up. Take action and claim what is yours from the universe. It is essential that you actively pursue your dreams and hopes. There is no one to play that role for you. It is in your power to shape your destiny, so go ahead and do what you have to do. Before asking to receive, be sure to get rid of all the clutter within your mind and soul. Cleanse the negative energy, because this is the only path towards achieving a deeper connection to your higher self. You do not need all this noise. What you do need is to have an active contribution to your evolution. You set your mind on something and you do whatever it takes, persuading the universe that you are entitled to it.

Feminine Energy Manifestation Guided Meditation

A guided meditation that you can use to manifest your feminine energy is the following, but feel free to experiment with similar words of appreciation towards the universe. You should be relaxed, preferably in a place with which you are familiar and comfortable in. Use sage to clear the space and promote your meditation. Light some candles and sit quietly. This is a sacred ceremony, offering you the opportunity to reach your highest self. "Dear universe, I am worthy of receiving what I want in life. I am ready to enjoy the manifestation of my feminine energy. I want to have my purest desires fulfilled right away because I deserve them. May I receive everything I want for the common good of all women. It is my right to enjoy life to the fullest so as to benefit the world through my exceptional lifestyle. My desires come in perfect alignment with nature. I want to remain in harmony with Gaia and this is how I am able to achieve that. I deserve to feel happy."

As you can imagine, it is vital that you remain calm throughout the meditation. You need to control your breathing and set the pace, so that you reach within your feminine energy and request what is yours. Close your eyes, make sure that your muscles are relaxed and dive into the subconscious. You are aiming at an endless flow of energy. Find the perfect way to listen to your body and realize where that flow is directed. Keep your sense of calmness as you repeat the above positive affirmations. Feel the energy awakening and all those desires of yours slowly manifested before your eyes.

It all has to do with your beliefs. You need to be sure that you deserve what you are asking to manifest through your feminine energy. Unless you are confident that you are entitled to these claims, you will never manage to obtain them. It doesn't matter if you have spent all this time trying to shift your mindset. You ought to come across as super confident, absolutely certain of what you should enjoy in your life. This guided meditation is just giving you the vessel through which to express your inner thoughts.

This Is A Marathon, Not A Sprint

All this knowledge might make you want to dive right in and experience your true divine power to its full potential. However, this is not the best way to go. I understand why you are so excited, but you need to take it easy. There is so much more to master before you experiment with the impact of your divinity. You are so new to this that it is prudent to take a deep breath and remain calm. Let the universe work its magic, and you sit there relax and enjoy what comes next.

There is no shortcut to anywhere worth going, right? This is a wonderful thing to keep in mind the next time you are tempted to rush and push things. Instead, you need to practice the art of patience. It can be hard at times, but as soon as you have seen the benefits it offers, you will be grateful that you have taken things slowly. In the meantime, appreciate the moment and evaluate your progress. Track down all the changes that have taken place so far. Be appreciative of all the good things that have come your way. Cherish the special moments that you have experienced so far and get ready for the future thrills.

Think of where you were when you started this journey, and take a look at where you are now. You have managed to do all these amazing things, you have set the foundations for an even greater future life. You are now ready to reap the benefits of your choices. Nevertheless, change doesn't happen overnight and this is something you must come to terms with. There are several stages you should go through, before getting accustomed to that overwhelming power from within. You should tame this power and learn how to be in control. It takes time and real struggle to get there. So plan ahead, lay out your weapons, and structure a strategy that will pay off eventually.

You need to master the skills that you are beginning to obtain, and this comes through practice and ongoing education. Never should you believe that you are done with studying. Life is always filled with new potential, which you can only unlock when you read and comprehend new concepts. We are not meant to stay idle as life passes us by. On the contrary, we need to move along with it, evolve, and unravel the hidden mysteries ahead. Allow yourself the time to master what you have learned so far. Try out different meditations which will unlock the parts of your body, your mind, your soul. Read all about setting the right atmosphere, which will awaken the senses and allow you to relax, opening your inner self.

Accept reality for what it is, and do not ignore the facts. You have endless power for change, but this doesn't mean that you will be able to form reality exactly the way you want it from one moment to the next. The Law of Attraction doesn't work like that. You first have to change your mindset and then go ahead with receiving what you want in life. This is a huge step you need to take, so don't be impatient. Set realistic goals and build your truth, brick by brick. In this way, you will create a solid masterpiece that will not fall to pieces with the first strong wind.

No matter how many setbacks you have experienced, you should not give up. Persistence is the key to success. Even the most successful people in life have experienced failure. In fact, some of these failures have played a catalytic role in their later development. You must make use of everything you've got. Take that failure and use it to your advantage. Learn from it, so as not to make the same mistakes ever again. This is exceptional knowledge, coming straight from experience, and it will serve as your shield of protection in the future. Unless you have had a taste of failure, chances are that you will not have the chance to succeed.

If you are an athlete, think of enlightenment and your journey towards awakening your divine power as a marathon. Do you enjoy running? If you try to sprint in a marathon, eventually you will come to the realization that you are wasting your energy and you have been laboring under false pretenses. The best strategy is to preserve your energy, and stick to your end goal. Maintain your power, find your ideal pace, and make sure that you keep up with the rhythm. This is going to bring you to the finish line sooner than anticipated!

AFTERWORD

OK, now what? Are you supposed to go on with your life, like your awakening has never taken place? Now that you have had a taste of your divine power, what are you meant to do? These are questions that must be running through your mind all the time. It is perfectly understandable, since what you have experienced is a true revelation. You have been awakened. You have managed to experience what only a few women do in their life. This means that you are special and must make good use of these special traits of yours. After having discovered something as mind blowing as this, it makes sense that you feel at a loss. "Where am I going from here?", "Which is the next step I should take?" and "Is this really happening to me?" are some of the questions you need to come up with answers right away.

I totally get it; you have been overwhelmed by emotion. It is like everything in your life is beginning to make sense. You are not the insecure woman that you once were. Fear does not define you any more. On the contrary, you have realize the magnitude of power that you hold within you and it makes your heart beat faster. You are most likely finding it hard to concentrate on anything but your recent transcendental experience. By now, you have probably played the same

AFTERWORD

thing over and over again in your mind, trying to discover even more details and savor every moment. I can't blame you. I was in shock when I found out about my true calling, and it took me a while to bounce back and resume my ordinary life.

Obviously, you are not expected to figure it all out from one day to the next. There is a learning curve, which you are about to follow. Every day, you will discover new things that you knew nothing about. Think of it as landing on a new planet, and trying to discover what lies out there. You cannot just start walking and walking until you have covered the entire planet, can you? That would turn out to be disastrous, as you would exhaust yourself and not have the clarity required to interpret the signs. Step by step, you must lay out your plans and figure out the best way to cover as much distance as possible each time.

This is earth shattering news that you have found; no one would be able to relax and just go out and about with their daily routine. It is impossible to go sit in front of a computer and do some data entry, or start answering the phone, without wanting to shout about your transformation. You have communicated with your inner goddess, finding just a small fraction of your power. Now you need to put this into perspective. You cannot change your life radically because it would throw you off guard. What you can do is to take baby steps, and read, and then read some more about what is happening to you. In this book, I hope I have given you the answers to all your questions, but you must continue your education for life.

It is important to stick to your routine and incorporate this immense change into your life in a way that does not mess with your reality check. Otherwise, you could be looking at social isolation. If you compare this experience to anything else you have ever lived so far, there will be a huge distance between them. However, you should not underestimate what has brought you to the place you are now. Do not forget about the people who have stood by your side. They deserve to be happy by your side, so don't exclude them from your life. On the other hand, those who have criticized and made fun of your beliefs do not belong anywhere near you.

THE WORLD IS YOUR OYSTER

...and you are the pearl. Life is full of surprises and you are ready to face the world with a different mindset. You are divine, you are sacred, you have been chosen to bless the earth and communicate with the universe. There is divinity within you, your inner goddess is inviting you to experience greatness. What is holding you back? Take that opportunity and make the most of it. Everyday should be a celebration of your unique nature. You are equipped to take on the world, pursuing your dreams and hopes until you instill life into them.

Take a look at the mirror and tell me what you see. I see an empowered woman, who is eager to discover all the hidden truths in life. You are thirsty for knowledge and you want to create, nurture, support and relish. There is nothing to stop you from your course. You are determined to survive and thrive against all odds. Your goal is to spread the word to others, letting women know just how powerful they really are. It is in your hands. You have the ability to influence more females into exploring their divine feminine power. This is your calling. This is your destiny. Enjoy being in the spotlight because you deserve it. Enjoy letting others walk in your shoes and follow your lead. You have earned it.

You are free to fly away in searches, discover uncharted lands, delve in crisp waters, and explore the vastness of the ocean. Nothing can stand in the way. It is sheer power that is guiding you, along with the enlightenment of deep knowledge from eternity. Take a look at the sun, the stars and the moon. Observe how great they are, shining on their own. They don't need anyone else to validate them. Instead, they know their true value and they never underestimate who they are. Imagine the infinite, the ancient power that has survived through millennia. You are part of this mystical truth. You are part of the universe, in perfect sync with its power.

The world is your oyster, because you are powerful and extraordinary. You are able to chart your own course, decide where you want to go and what you want to do. There is no restriction. There is no one who can deny your immense power and limitless possibilities in

AFTERWORD

life. Rather than finding excuses to reject your options and narrow them down to what is familiar, you need to expand and broaden your horizons. Step out of your comfort zone. You have not come all this way to simply settle for what others dictate. On the contrary, you have always been a visionary. Never has your mind rested; you always try to learn more and discover what remains hidden in the darkness.

With the shocking revelation that you are a sacred entity, directly connected to your ancient spirit, how can you change your beliefs and live life differently? Reach out to the world, revealing your secrets and connecting to others who are experiencing the same things, as you do so. Your life is about to change more than you know. Train your brain, acknowledge the changes, and figure out how to control your inner energy. This is the pathway to true awareness. Then, you will be unstoppable. You will have the power to flow through the universe, calling out nature's most precious elements to bathe you with wisdom, love, light and hope. An ethereal creature like you is entitled to all these magnificent things in life. You just have to reach out and take what is rightfully yours. Brace yourself, because this is going to be a life-changing experience!

A Heartfelt Farewell

Congratulations, dear females! You have successfully completed your path towards enlightenment and it is time to reveal the next step. How are you moving forward with your life now that you have stepped into your divine power? Throughout the book, I have tried to describe in detail every single part of the awakening process. I know that the journey is going to be different for every single one of you ladies. However, there is one thing I can promise right here, right now. If you follow the steps that I have laid out in these sections, you will get much closer to your inner goddess than ever before. This is an accomplishment on its own.

I hope that you have already come to realize just how unique your true self is. It would be an honor for me to hear that you have appreciated your feminine side a little more, thanks to some of the things I said. You need to be aware of your special higher self and always treat yourself right. There are ways to reach deep within your soul and discover your feminine energy. Over time, you will learn how to master this flow of energy, so that you can contain it and use it exactly the way you want. This wonderful immense source of energy will offer you endless possibilities in life, so you should keep your eyes open and make use of that.

I wish you all love in life. You deserve a life filled with love and care, so make sure that you surround yourself with people who are generous. More than that, I wish you light in your life; may it bathe you with its beneficial properties. The pure light shining over you and offering you all those warm feelings comes from awareness and curiosity. I hope that this is the light that guides you through your journey. This is going to be an extraordinary experience for you. And above all, I wish you courage. There will be times when you feel like giving up. As I told you earlier in the book, awakening your feminine energy is not all roses and flowers. So you will need all the courage you can have, so as to endure the pain, and make it through the hard work and strenuous effort.

This experience will only make you stronger and more enlightened. Do not shy away from the challenge. Read through the different sections, taking in all the details that form your guiding light. This will be your beacon, even when you feel lost on your journey. Turn back to the pages that deal with specific aspects of your awakening and try to understand them. This is hard-earned knowledge, which I was lucky enough to document and pass on to you. Feel free to read again and again, until you fully perceive the concept of reaching your divine feminine. Your transformation has already begun, which is an outstanding thing to consider. This is something you should be proud of. Not many women have been blessed to live the way you do. So it is your duty to take on the challenge and make the most of it every single day.

Take a moment and contemplate what you have achieved so far. You have come a long way and I couldn't be prouder of you, girls. Now, everything is changing. Your life will improve drastically now that you have grasped the full potential of your inner power. All this empirical knowledge is available to you now that you have completed this book.

AFTERWORD

Reach out and take what you want, because your time has come. It is your moment to shine and radiate with a blissful glow, showing the world what you are made of. You are sacred. You are unique. You are wonderful. Good luck on your journey, and I wish you all the best...which I am sure you are bound to experience, now that you have completed your goddess energy awakening!

REFERENCES

Create Balance And Harmony Using The Law Of Polarity. (2016, December). www.Magzter.com. https://www.magzter.com/article/Lifestyle/OMTimes-Magazine/Create-Balance-And-Harmony-Using-TheLaw-Of-Polarity

dc20462. (2017). Glow Woman Women. In *Pixabay*. https://pixabay.com/photos/glow-woman-women-s-silhouette-sea-2826154/

Devanath. (2016). Lotus Natural Water. In *Pixabay*. https://pixabay.com/photos/lotus-natural-water-meditation-zen-1205631/

FelixMittermeier. (2017). Milky Way Starry Sky Night. In *Pixabay*. https://pixabay.com/photos/milky-way-starry-sky-night-sky-star-2695569/

Fotorech. (2017). Sky Freedom Happiness. In *Pixabay*. https://pixabay.com/photos/sky-freedom-happiness-relieved-2667455/

Free Photos. (2014). Summerfield Woman Girl. In *Pixabay*. https://pixabay.com/photos/summerfield-woman-girl-sunset-336672/

Free Photos. (2015). Sparkler Holding Hands. In *Pixabay*. https://pixabay.com/photos/sparkler-holding-hands-firework-677774/

Free Photos. (2016). Person Mountain Top Achieve. In *Pixabay*. https://pixabay.com/photos/person-mountain-top-achieve-1245959/

REFERENCES

geralt. (2019). Self Love Heart Diary. In *Pixabay*. https://pixabay.com/photos/self-love-heart-diary-hand-keep-3969644/

Gorbachevsergeyfoto. (2018). Woman Portrait Girl. In *Pixabay*. https://pixabay.com/photos/woman-portrait-girl-people-model-3287956/

Hans. (2016). Girl Person Child Summer. In *Pixabay*. https://pixabay.com/photos/girl-person-child-summer-dress-1469748/

HNewberry. (2016). Goddess Female Pagan. In *Pixabay*. https://pixabay.com/photos/goddess-female-pagan-magic-lady-1500599/

Katerina Knizakova. (2017). Model Red Weed Field. In *Pixabay*. https://pixabay.com/photos/model-red-weed-field-green-plant-1955528/

kudybadorota. (2018). Girl Daydreaming Horse. In *Pixabay*. https://pixabay.com/photos/girl-daydreaming-horse-daydream-3551832/

Leninscape. (2017). Yoga Outdoor Woman. In *Pixabay*. https://pixabay.com/photos/yoga-outdoor-woman-pose-young-2176668/

msandersmusic. (2016). Stained Glass Spiral Circle. In *Pixabay*. https://pixabay.com/photos/stained-glass-spiral-circle-pattern-1181864/

netage. (n.d.). The Da Vinci Code & Mary Magdalene |. Netage.Org. https://netage.org/the-da-vinci-code-mary-magdalene/

NRThaele. (2017). Girl Freedom Climbing. In *Pixabay*. https://pixabay.com/photos/girl-freedom-climbing-hiking-1955797/

Paulo Coelho - Wikiquote. (n.d.). En.Wikiquote.Org. Retrieved September 15, 2020, from https://en.wikiquote.org/wiki/Paulo_Coelho

Peterson, J. (2020, March 4). *Jordan Peterson explains the yin yang symbol*. Logo Design Love. https://www.logodesignlove.com/yin-yang-symbol

Piro4d. (2017). Feng Shui Stones Coast. In *Pixabay*. https://pixabay.com/photos/feng-shui-stones-coast-spirituality-1960783/

Qimono. (2018). Drop Splash Drip. In *Pixabay*. https://pixabay.com/photos/drop-splash-drip-water-liquid-wet-3698073/

Silviarita. (2017). Young Woman Girl Umbrella. In *Pixabay*. https://pixabay.com/photos/young-woman-girl-umbrella-rain-out-2268348/

Sweetlouise. (2017). Necklace Heart Stones White. In *Pixabay*. https://pixabay.com/photos/necklace-heart-stones-white-gold-2149668/

The Law Of Attraction—Discover How to Improve Your Life. (n.d.).

REFERENCES

The Law Of Attraction. Retrieved September 15, 2020, from https://www.thelawofattraction.com/

Wikipedia Contributors. (2019, April 27). *Self-fulfilling prophecy*. Wikipedia; Wikimedia Foundation. https://en.wikipedia.org/wiki/Self-fulfilling_prophecy

YOUR FEEDBACK IS VALUED

We would like to be so bold as to ask for an act of kindness from you. If you read and enjoyed our book/s, would you please consider leaving an honest review on Amazon or audible? As an independent publishing group, your feedback means the absolute world to us. We read every single review we receive and would love to hear your thoughts, as each piece of feedback helps us serve you better. Your feedback may also impact others across the globe, helping them discover powerful knowledge they can implement in their lives to give them hope and self-empowerment. Wishing you empowerment, courage, and wisdom on your journey.

If you have read or listened to any of our books and would be so kind as to review them, you can do so by clicking the 'learn more' tab under the book's picture on our website:

https://ascendingvibrations.net/books

YOUR FEEDBACK IS VALUED

Why not join our Facebook community and discuss your spiritual path with like-minded seekers?

We would love to hear from you!

Go here to join the 'Ascending Vibrations' community:
   bit.ly/ascendingvibrations

YOUR *BONUS* AUDIOBOOK IS READY

Download the 6+ Hour Audiobook *'Divine Feminine Energy (Manifesting for Women & Feminine Energy Awakening - 2 in 1 Collection)'* Instantly for **FREE.**

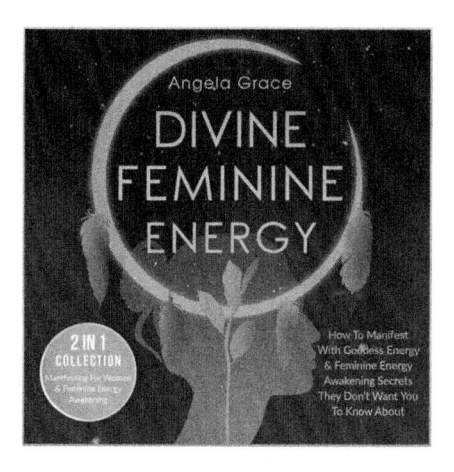

If you love listening to audio books on-the-go, I have great news for you. You can download the audio book version of *'Divine Feminine Energy'* for **FREE** just by signing up for a **FREE** 30-day audible trial! See below for more details.

YOUR *BONUS* AUDIOBOOK IS READY

Audible trial benefits

As an audible customer, you'll receive the below benefits with you 30-day free trial:

- Free audible copy of this book
- After the trial, you will get 1 credit each month to use on any audiobook
- Your credits automatically roll over to the next month if you don't use them
- Choose from over 400,000 titles
- Listen anywhere with the audible app across multiple devices
- Make easy, no hassle exchanges of any audiobook you don't love
- Keep your audiobooks forever, even if you cancel your membership
- And much more

Go to the links below to get started:
Go here for AUDIBLE US: bit.ly/divinefeminineenergy
Go here for AUDIBLE UK: bit.ly/divinefeminineenergyuk

Printed in Great Britain
by Amazon